TEN
MODERN POETS

TEN
MODERN POETS

by Rica Brenner

Essay Index Reprint Series

Originally published by:
HARCOURT, BRACE AND COMPANY

BOOKS FOR LIBRARIES PRESS, INC.
Freeport, New York

To

C. B.

who has waited, sympathized, and helped
with something much more than appreciation
this book is dedicated

PREFACE

There is but one unfailing method of reading poetry,
whether it was written yesterday or centuries ago—
that of the bee in the blossom, or, as the Puritans
might prefer to put it, that of puss in the dairy. We
need but take pleasure in it, all the pleasure, delight,
happiness, that it has to bestow, and that we are
capable of receiving.
—WALTER DE LA MARE, "The Reading
of Contemporary Poetry."

THIS BOOK has been written not with the desire to
evaluate ten poets, to dissect them and their work,
and to assign them to respective—and dustily forgotten—
places in the history of English literature; it has been
written rather with the hope that through it an increased
pleasure might accrue to those who read these poets'
verses. Readers already acquainted with the poets may
find in it biographical background and suggested points of
view that will, perhaps, round out their understanding
and so increase their enjoyment. New readers will find a
cordial introduction to the delights that await them.

For the choice of the five American poets and the five
English poets who are thus presented, no apology is
needed. That must be reserved for the failure to include
others, the omission of whom is due only to the physical
limitations of the book. Some explanation, however, may

be given of the reasons underlying the choice and the manner of treatment.

All the poets, save one, are living and so, chronologically, are "modern." The only exception, Amy Lowell, who died as recently as 1925, was one of the acknowledged leaders of the "modern movement" and was in her writings so avowed a formulator and follower of liberal poetic principles that nothing could excuse her omission from a group of modern poets.

It is, indeed, this liberalized intellectual attitude, and not the judgment of the calendar, that must determine whether or not a poet is modern. Yet it must not be understood that a poet is a "modern poet" because he holds some particular philosophy of life. His philosophy identifies him primarily as a man, not as a poet. As a matter of fact, any one writing today must be touched in one way or another by the power of contemporary composite thought; and, on the other hand, contemporary life exhibits so many varieties of conduct and of beliefs that almost any and every system of philosophy may to some degree be regarded as modern. The essence of today's philosophy lies in that very eclecticism.

But if it is not by his answer to the problems of life, by what, then, is a poet's modernity to be judged? That is to be determined by his attitude toward poetry. The freedom that characterizes other fields of intellectual activity must characterize this attitude, too. A poet, to be modern, must very definitely rebel against the idea that the past has defined for all time the material and methods of poetry. For him, poetry has acquired a wider field than it knew in the past; his subject is not limited by old conceptions of the poetic. He finds poetry not only where others before him have found it—and almost exhausted the vein; he is free to discover it where he, and he alone, wills.

He feels himself equally free to present it in the manner which he deems most suitable. But in stepping beyond the bounds laid down by the old conventions of poetic diction and of prosody, he does not throw away all rules. He writes most definitely according to a code of regulations. These rules he has evolved out of his poetry; he has not permitted them to dictate his poetry to him. At the same time, he does not blindly and stubbornly reject what the past has to offer. He adapts to his own use both the measured beat of the older verse and the less distinct, but none the less certain, rhythmic pulse of the newer. Purpose and appropriateness, alone, decide his choice.

The modern poet, free to experiment, is characterized by his inquisitiveness toward life and art, by his desire to find truth for himself, by his consciousness of freedom and of individuality of expression. In this manner are the ten poets of this volume modern poets. Differing one from the other in temperament, in interests, in methods, they are yet alike in their independence of individuality.

It is, of course, possible to talk circuitously about poets and their characteristics without quoting from their writings. But so much point is given, so much vividness added, when their own words may be used! So, grateful ac-

knowledgment is made to the poets and their publishers
for the privilege of quotation.

To Mr. Housman, personally, and to his authorized
publisher, Henry Holt and Company, my sincere thanks
are due. For the privilege of quoting from "The Two-
Sided Man," "How the Whale Got His Throat," "Pha-
raoh and the Sergeant," "Recessional," "White Man's
Burden," "The Islanders," "My Boy Jack," "To Tommy
Atkins," "Tommy," and "The Gipsy Trail," I thank Mr.
Kipling, personally, and his publisher, Doubleday, Doran
and Company. The selections from the writings of Amy
Lowell are used by permission of, and special arrangement with, Houghton Mifflin and Company, for whose
kindness I am grateful. Miss Millay's unnamed sonnet,
Sonnet V, is quoted, by permission, from *Renascence and
Other Poems*, published by Harper and Brothers, copyright 1917 by Edna St. Vincent Millay. My appreciation
of the permission to quote from the other writers is due,
and is acknowledged, as follows: for permission to quote
from Walter de la Mare, to Henry Holt and Company;
Robert Frost, Henry Holt and Company; John Masefield, The Macmillan Company; Alfred Noyes, Frederick A. Stokes Company; Edwin Arlington Robinson, to
Charles Scribner's Sons for quotations from *Children of
the Night* and *Town Down the River*, to The Macmillan
Company for quotations from *Captain Craig, The Man
Against the Sky, Merlin, The Three Taverns, Avon's
Harvest, Roman Bartholow, The Man Who Died Twice,
Dionysus in Doubt*, and *Tristram*, to Thomas A. Seltzer
for quotations from *Lancelot*; Carl Sandburg, to Henry

Holt and Company for quotations from *Chicago Poems*
and *Corn Huskers,* to Harcourt, Brace and Company for
quotations from *Smoke and Steel, Slabs of the Sunburnt
West,* and *Good Morning, America.*

This pleasant record of gratitude would seem to omit
those whom I should most like to thank. But they,
through whom came the initial impetus to write this book
and the patient and generous assistance in developing it,
know without this acknowledgment that I am grateful.

R. B.

August, 1929.

CONTENTS

ILLUSTRATIONS

ROBERT FROST

ROBERT FROST

A LITTLE girl and her ten-year-old brother had invented a game. First, they would hold up a nickel and shout "San Francisco." Then they would hold up a penny and, with supreme scorn and contempt for the coin of lesser value, mutter "Boston."[1] The boy was Robert Frost, who was later to become the poet of that New England which, at ten, he despised.

It was natural enough that the boy's thoughts should turn lovingly back to the Western home which he had been forced to leave because of his father's death. But it was also natural enough that the boy should grow to love New England, where, at his grandfather's farm, he with his mother and his sister had found a new home. For the return to the East was a return to the land of his paternal ancestors; and the New England strain, which had begun when Nicholas Frost, in 1632, sailed from England and arrived in Maine, was too strong not to exert itself in the ninth generation of American Frosts.

To understand Frost, one must realize this background of tradition. Furthermore, one must realize that for him there was no meek acceptance of the past; for he was too

[1] Related by Gorham B. Munson in *Robert Frost: A Study in Sensibility and Good Sense*, George H. Doran Co., New York.

3

much influenced by a highly individualized father who, disliking New England, had gone to San Francisco to live an independent life. This combination of the individual's sense of the past and his determination to create his own tradition is fundamental to Frost's poetry. "I believe in tradition," he says, "and accident and a bit of an idea bothering tradition"; and again, he says in "Into My Own":

I do not see why I should e'er turn back,
Or those should not set forth upon my track
To overtake me, who should miss me here
And long to know if still I held them dear.

They would not find me changed from him they knew—
Only more sure of all I thought was true.

For seven generations the history of the Frost family centered in a few Maine and New Hampshire villages. Nicholas, the founder of the family, lost his wife and his daughter in a fight with the Indians. His son Charles was killed by the Indians in 1697 because of their resentment of the white men's treachery, in which Frost had played a reluctant part. William Prescott Frost, a Frost of the seventh generation and the poet's grandfather, moved to Massachusetts and became an overseer in a mill in Lawrence. His wife was a feminist, and believed so strongly in women's rights that she was able to institute a household régime in which half the housework was done by her husband.

It may have been from this strong-willed mother that William Prescott, Jr., inherited his own independence of thought and action. He was sent to Harvard; but after graduation, instead of settling in Lawrence and practicing law as his family had hoped he would do, he decided to leave home and to create an existence for himself. His revolt against New England finally led him to San Francisco. His journey there, however, was interrupted by a stop at Lewiston, Pennsylvania, where he taught school and where he married another teacher, Isabelle Moody, a young girl from Edinburgh.

The two set out for San Francisco. There Frost became editor of *The Bulletin,* a Democratic paper. And there on March 26, 1875, Robert was born. The name Robert Lee was chosen to suggest the father's sympathy with the Southern principle of States Rights, a principle to which few dyed-in-the-wool New Englanders adhered.

The San Francisco in which Robert grew up was a lawless place. To men there bullets were more familiar than walking-sticks. Political campaigns were accompanied by wild celebrations. In the campaign of 1884, Robert's father ran for the position of tax collector. He failed of election, however, in spite of the fact that Robert had faithfully performed his duty of distributing campaign literature among the voters in the city saloons. In the following year, the boy's father died. He left so little money that the family were unable to maintain their own home and were obliged to return to the East to live with the Frost grandfather.

The life that began at this point, a New England life, is the one most definitely reflected in Frost's poetry. His interests were identified with Lawrence. His schooling was got at the local schools. At high school his work was so good that there seemed no doubt of his being chosen class valedictorian. But—and this is of future significance—a rival to his honors appeared in the person of Elinor White, a descendant of Peregrine White of the *Mayflower*. Elinor was doing the four years' work in two and a half years— and was doing it so well that, at the end of the school course, her average tied with Robert's. The difficulty of choosing the valedictorian was settled by letting Robert deliver the address while on the program the names of both were printed as filling the honored position.

During these school years, Frost's interest in literature grew. Up to the age of fourteen his favorite book had been *Tom Brown's School Days*. Now he began to read William Cullen Bryant, Edgar Allan Poe, Edward Rowland Sill. He read a little of Shelley and of Keats but did not find in them the satisfaction that he found in the others. With his discovery of the poets, he began his own attempts at verse writing. When he was seventeen, he sold his first poem, "My Butterfly," to *The Independent* for fifteen dollars. William Hays Ward, the editor of the magazine, tried to induce the young poet to modify his style. But Frost was convinced that his literary method must be his own creation; and so he refused to be influenced by editorial suggestions.

This same determination to create his own pattern manifested itself in other than poetical matters. The demands of formal collegiate training became irksome and, after a couple of months, Frost left Dartmouth College, in which he had enrolled. There followed years of varied experi-

ences, of one kind of job or another, of efforts to find satisfying work and the time to write satisfying poems. During
this period Frost was a bobbin boy at a Lawrence mill—
and read Shakespeare in his rest periods! He made shoes.
He taught Latin at his mother's school in Lawrence. He
became a reporter for *The Sentinel,* the town paper, and
wrote articles for what would today be called a "column."
Then, in 1895, he married Elinor White, his rival for
valedictorian honors. Even marriage, however, failed to
make him a settled young man. Two years later he resumed his schooling and registered at Harvard, where his
interest lay particularly in Latin, Greek, and philosophy.
But in spite of intellectual stimulation and the pleasure
which he took in a number of his courses, two years was
the limit of his Harvard stay.

Finally, in 1900, his grandfather—kindly, tolerant, but
wondering why the young man couldn't buckle down to
something steady—bought him a farm. Then began that
life of farming and the leisurely creating of poems that,
except for a few brief interruptions, has continued to the
present. The farm, an $1,800 one, was situated in Derry,
in the southeast corner of New Hampshire. Derry Village
was an old, settled, unprogressive community with a few
long-established but small industries and with Pinkerton
Academy as its center of education and culture.

Frost's farm, like so many New England farms, was a
hard one from which to make a living. Nor can it be
imagined that Frost, whose mind was filled with rhythms,
and rhymes, and a fresh theory of poetry, was using the
most scientific or the most generally accepted methods of

farming. He confesses to having milked cows at ten o'clock at night so that he need not rise at the early hour at which orthodox farmers milk orthodox cows. In "The Star-Splitter" he describes an unsuccessful farmer in words that might apply to himself:

> Busy outdoors by lantern-light with something
> I should have done by daylight, and indeed,
> After the ground is frozen, I should have done
> Before it froze.

Such haphazard farming methods, however, do not pay the bills of a growing family. In 1905, Robert Frost found that he had exhausted his credit with the village butcher. He applied for a position at Pinkerton Academy; and, largely because of a favorable impression he had created through a poem "The Tuft of Flowers" read at the Men's Club of the Central Congregational Church, he was appointed. At first, on the part of the older students and some of the faculty, there was opposition to the new, informally educated teacher. But this instructor had something to give to his pupils. He was interested in their activities. He gave judicious advice to *The Critic*, the school publication. He coached plays. He helped celebrate football victories; and for one over Sanborn Seminary, he wrote a triumphal song:

> In the days of Captain John,
> Sanborn Sem had nothing on
> Pinkerton, Pinkerton.[2]

[2] Quoted in Munson's *Robert Frost*.

But, more than all else, he was interested in his students as individuals. As there was nothing stereotyped about them, so there was nothing stereotyped about his teaching. His interest, his fresh viewpoint, his stimulating ability made him one of the school's best teachers. Thus it happened that when Mr. Silver, the principal of Pinkerton, was appointed head of the New Hampshire State Normal School at Plymouth, he asked Frost to go with him. Here Frost taught English and psychology during the school year of 1911-1912.

His school work, however confining it might prove at times, still gave him opportunity to write. His poems made the rounds of the magazines, *Scribner's*, *Century* and the *Atlantic Monthly*. There was an occasional acceptance, particularly by *The Forum* and by *Youth's Companion*—enough acceptances, evidently, to give Frost the courage to set out definitely and with steady devotion to a life of poetry.

He sold his farm and in September 1912 sailed for England. There he settled in the little town of Beaconsfield, in "leafy Bucks," the lovely county of Buckinghamshire close to London.

About this time forces were gathering which were to bring about a revival of poetry. In October, in America, Harriet Monroe brought out the first issue of *Poetry, A Magazine of Verse*. In England, as in America, writers were experimenting with new subjects and with new forms for poetry. In London, Harold Munro was holding receptions and readings in his Poetry Book Shop. Frost, quite uninvited and purely by chance, happened in on one of these evenings of poetry. "I see by your shoes you are an American," some one addressed him and then introduced him to Ezra Pound. It was Ezra Pound who was to write the first review of *A Boy's Will*, Frost's first volume of poetry, which had just been accepted for publication by David Nutt.

In *A Boy's Will*, Frost collected the best of the poems he had been writing during his years of self-training, and with prose comments sought to connect them into a unified expression of a boy's social and intellectual growth. The poems are essentially subjective and personal.

In 1914 *North of Boston* appeared, published by the same English firm as had published the first volume. In this book occur those vivid portrayals of New England scene and people which are done in the manner that is typically Frost's. The book was well received; but the financial return from the sales was small. At Little Iddens, a farm in Gloucestershire, Frost resumed farming to supplement his literary earnings. Here he had as neighbors the poets Wilfred Wilson Gibson and Lascelles Abercrombie.

Meanwhile the great war had broken out. Poets became soldiers overnight. The arts must wait on war. England was no longer a quiet place for peaceful contemplation and the writing of poetry.

In March 1915 Frost left England to return to America, which had not yet entered the war. The day his boat landed, and entirely by accident, Frost came upon the February 20 number of a new magazine, *The New Republic*. In it was a review by Amy Lowell of *North of*

Boston, which had meanwhile found an American publisher.

Amy Lowell's appreciation was enthusiastic. She discovered in the poems a true American note. "Mr. Frost is only expatriated in a physical sense," she wrote. "Living in England, he is, nevertheless, saturated with New England. For not only is his work New England in subject, it is so in technique. . . . It is certainly the most American volume of poetry which has appeared in some time."

Miss Lowell was to be the herald of a number of admirers. In the *Atlantic Monthly* for August 1915, the critic Edward Garnett wrote an influential review in which he said, "An authentic original force speaks in *North of Boston*." Honors began to come to the poet. In 1916, he was chosen Phi Beta Kappa poet at Harvard, and there read "The Axe-Helve," which was to appear later in *New Hampshire*. He was made an honorary member of the P.E.N. club, an association of writers. He was chosen Poet Laureate of Vermont.

Since 1915, in addition to a volume of selected poems, three more books of poems have appeared: *Mountain Interval* in 1916; *New Hampshire* in 1923; and in 1928, *West-Running Brook*. *Mountain Interval* continues the tradition of *North of Boston*. It contains such crisp, dramatic portraits as are found in the earlier book; and it contains, too, a number of shorter poems taking their inspiration from the country Frost had grown to love, yet written in a mood different from the personal one of *A Boy's Will*.

In *New Hampshire,* these two types of poems are again present but treated with greater sureness and deftness. The plan of the book is amusing, if not particularly important. The opening poem is the one that gives the book its title. It sings, in a not too serious manner, the charms of New Hampshire as a state of samples:

> Just specimens is all New Hampshire has,
> One each of everything as in a show-case
> Which naturally she doesn't care to sell.

The other poems in the volume Frost chooses to call "Notes" and "Grace Notes" to the opening one.

In *West-Running Brook,* his most recent book, there is much more of the revelation of the personal Robert Frost expressed in compact, sharp-chiseled verse. There are, somewhat surprisingly, several poems prompted by ideas and events of long ago, poems like "A Peck of Gold" and "Once by the Pacific," for example, that are reminiscent of his early California life. But for the larger number of poems, the poet has found his inspiration in his beloved New England.

It was in New Hampshire, on a farm at Franconia, that Frost first settled on his return to America. His farm life, however, was to be interrupted by several years of teaching. In 1916-1919, Frost, though without a college diploma, was a member of the Amherst faculty, entrusted with the task of teaching his students a love of creative literature. A critical professor elsewhere wrote, "The general impression is that it is an experiment which can not succeed. Frost is a countrified poet with a new system of metrics which I can not understand."

In 1921, the "countrified poet" was invited to fill the Fellowship in the Arts at Michigan University. The appointment, made originally for one year, was extended to two; and again, in 1925, Frost was invited back to the University to hold a life fellowship in poetry.

But the call of New England was too strong. Frost resigned his college position and in 1926 he returned permanently to his home in South Shaftesbury, Vermont, which he had purchased in 1920. From there, as an itinerant teacher, he makes occasional visits to colleges and occasional lecture tours. But his chief interests are farming and poetry.

A writer in *The Survey* [3] draws a picture of the Frost of Franconia days:

"I see him dressed in a gray suit, a gray cap snatched down over a finely-shaped head, shaggy, granite-streaked, hair straggling out; blue eyes, twinkling blue eyes with whimsical crinkles playing hide and seek around the corners, hooded with quizzical eyebrows; below, a droll, friendly, engaging expression, yet with something elusive about it as though he viewed life with an amused detachment."

The picture—now transferred to South Shaftesbury—may be further developed: [4]

"Frost's body makes little impression on one who meets

[3] Paul L. Benjamin, "The Poet of Neighborliness," *The Survey*, Nov. 27, 1920.
[4] "The Literary Spotlight," *The Bookman*, May 1923.

him for the first time. It is the eyes; bright blue, steady,
gentle yet canny, two vivid lights in a face that is otherwise gray. . . .

"He is a dignified figure as he sits on the back porch
of his stone farmhouse on a rise of the road near South
Shaftesbury, Vermont. . . . The family have made a
fountain in the backyard, which slopes by bushy meadow-
lands away to the Green Mountains. Frost works late into
the night and sleeps far into the morning. He likes to
walk. He likes to sit watching that fountain and letting
his mind play along its rising and falling waters. Occasional visitors there are, hospitably received."

One of his own literary neighbors, Dorothy Canfield, as
if to emphasize the fact that Robert Frost can not be
thought of away from the New England which he has
made his home, describes the Shaftesbury house: [5]

"A long time the house had stood there, about a hundred and thirty years, and nothing unusual had happened
to it. But it is the kind of house that can afford to wait,
and turn all the riper and sweeter for it, built as it is of
stone from out its own home ground. . . . To us his
house looks not at all grim or sombre, but homelike and
strong and cheerful and protecting, when we look up at it
as we start to climb Peleg Cole's hill, and see it at the top,
standing wide-roofed and substantial, with its old lilac
and syringa bushes, and the lily-of-the-valley bed, earlier
to bloom than in any other of our gardens, because of the
sun's warmth reflected from the grey stone walls against
which it is planted."

[5] "Robert Frost's Hilltop," *The Bookman*, December 1926.

Frost's life, it is evident, has not been an adventurous one. And so his poetry is not the poetry of adventure, nor yet of any unusual experience. Even the family traditions of ancestral fights with the Indians, even the glamorous San Francisco days, the life in England, and the upheaval of the great war enter almost not at all into his poems. His is the poetry—touched by genius—of everyday life, of the "common in experience, uncommon in writing."

This phrase is part of a formula which Frost himself used to explain different kinds of writing:

Uncommon in experience—uncommon in writing.

Common in experience—common in writing.

Uncommon in experience—common in writing.

Common in experience—uncommon in writing.

The last, he would insist, is the proper material and method for literature.

From this generalization, Frost has worked out and explained his theory of poetry. The common in experience includes not only subject matter, but mood, tone, and—very particularly—words. Modern poetry uses the words of common speech, of the trades, and of the shops—what Frost calls the "unmade words"; and by the "making touch" transforms them into things of beauty and of poetic significance. Modern poets, Frost once explained in a lecture, must create their own poetic diction and must reject those words which poets in the past have made poetical. "*Alien*," he said, "should not be used in poetry. Since Keats wrote 'She stood in tears amid the alien corn,' no poet has the right to use that word except in connection with Ellis Island."

The title of one of his own books illustrates this point. What might be more prosaic than the geographical, railroad term "North of Boston"? Yet what title actually succeeds in conveying more significant beauty? Frost's "making touch" has transformed this phrase.

"Poetry," Frost defines as "words that have become deeds," and "a complete poem" as "one where an emotion has found its thought and the thought has found the words."

With these ideals, Frost definitely set out on his creative way and the result has been something distinctly his. His first poems, as one may find in *A Boy's Will*, contained a few samples of traditional poetic diction, like "But I am fain to list," "The cagèd yellow bird," "the bruisèd plant." But the wrenched accents, the poetical *o'ers* and *perchances* soon disappear: and in the later volumes, one finds the uncommon writing of the common in experience.

The word *experience* must not be ignored. For Frost has experienced his poems. They are poems of observation, inspired by some one he has seen or by something he has noticed. They very definitely are not the poems of revery or of abstract fancy.

Discarding the earlier "poetic diction," Frost expresses his thoughts in the words which he has heard his neighbors use. There is, however, no effort at dialect, no straining after narrow local color. In "The Death of the Hired Man," an old laborer returns to the farm where he has formerly worked. The farmer's wife begs her husband to find something for the old man to do in order to save his self-respect.

ROBERT FROST

"He meant to clear the upper pasture, too.
That sounds like something you have heard before?
Warren, I wish you could have heard the way
He jumbled everything. I stopped to look
Two or three times—he made me feel so queer—
To see if he was talking in his sleep."

These are the words of common speech. But, in addition, this is the meter and the rhythm of common speech. Some of Frost's poems, it is true, are lyric in meter, written in rhyming quatrains or couplets. But the characteristic Frost meter is a free, elastic, blank verse, a blank verse that does not hesitate to substitute some variation from the classic iambic foot.

Mrs. Baptiste came in and rocked a chair
That had as many motions as the world:
One back and forward, in and out of shadow,
That got her nowhere; one more gradual,
Sideways, that would have run her on the stove
In time, had she not realized her danger
And caught herself up bodily, chair and all,
And set herself back where she started from.

Yet, in the use of usual words and meter, there is no sacrifice of beauty. In "The Death of the Hired Man," from which a quotation has already been made, there is a passage as lovely as one could wish:

Part of a moon was falling down the west,
Dragging the whole sky with it to the hills.
Its light poured softly in her lap. She saw

And spread her apron to it. She put out her hand
Among the harp-like morning-glory strings,
Taut with the dew from garden bed to eaves,
As if she played unheard the tenderness
That wrought on him beside her in the night.
"Warren," she said, "he has come home to die.
You needn't be afraid he'll leave you this time."

This is no isolated example. Its beauty is the very material
of which Frost makes all his poems.

With this simplicity, very possibly as a result of it, the
poet is able to achieve a vividness of impression. Consider,
for example, this quotation from "The Mountain":

The mountain held the town as in a shadow.
I saw so much before I slept there once:
I noticed that I missed stars in the west,
Where its black body cut into the sky.

A few details, simple and unelaborated, but clear-cut, build
up the unforgettable effect of a towering mass.

In this poem, a resident of the town has never climbed
the overshadowing mountain, which boasts a remarkable
spring, and from which there ought to be a breath-taking
view.

"I've always meant to go
And look myself, but you know how it is:
It doesn't seem so much to climb a mountain
You've worked around the foot of all your life."

A person who manifests such indifference to the things
about him is by no means extraordinary. It is people as

usual and as easily recognized as this who are the characters in Frost's poems: a family who makes its living picking berries, a young couple beginning a new home, Baptiste
who knew

> how to make a short job long
> For love of it, and yet not waste time either.

the worker in "The Death of the Hired Man," the ideal-
istic and unsuccessful farmer in "The Star-Splitter," the
nature lover in "The Self-Seeker." These are simple
people but very real ones.

Most of Frost's characters are men and women whose
lives have been formed by the demands that Nature
makes, men and women of small communities, of farms
—above all, of cold, poor New England farms. About
them are tradition and the molding influence of the past.
Rarely is there the suggestion of a hopeful future.

Yet there is in the poetry no overwhelming sense of
sadness. There is humor not only in occasional felicitous
phrases, but in Frost's general outlook upon life, as in
"The Bear" and "The Door in the Dark." And several
poems are frankly humorous in purpose. In "A Hundred
Collars," for example, a dignified professor,

> Though a great scholar, he's a democrat.
> If not at heart, at least on principle

is forced to share a small country hotel bedroom with
Lafe, an intoxicated reporter, who insists upon giving him
the collars which he himself has outgrown. Or there may
be the sheer exuberant good humor of a poem like

"Brown's Descent," which tells the story of how Farmer Brown, blown by the wind one wintry night, slips and slides down an icy hill to the valley two miles away.

Here, in addition to the humor, there is a revivifying of New England character in the stanzas beginning "Yankees are what they always were." These Yankee men and women Frost can put in dramatic situations created by deft, but quiet means. In "Snow," for example, the story of Meserve, a preacher of the Racker Sect, who is making his way home in a blinding snowstorm, the reader is held tense by the suggestion of some supernatural force, by the fears of the Coles, Meserve's temporary hosts. The reader lives with them; with them, he builds up in disturbed fancy the difficulties of Meserve's trip, the inevitability of his death in the storm. The fears are needless. A telephone call, which has inherent in it all the elements of supreme tragedy, announces the preacher's safe arrival home. With this matter-of-fact ending, the Coles exhibit a change of feeling toward Meserve; he loses the heroic qualities with which they had endowed him.

In "The Witch of Coös," there is manifest the same ability to tell a story. But in this case, there is a reversal of method; the story of a grim murder is suggested in terms and mood as calm as though they were recounting a walk down a country road. The Witch, a country woman who is known as a spiritualist, tells of a skeleton that one night rose from its cellar grave to wander through her house. As it came toward her, she struck its hand. The bone that broke off she keeps in her button-box. She was able to direct the skeleton's progress to the attic through

an open door, which she then shut and locked. But sometimes at night, the skeleton comes down the stairs to the
wall behind the headboard of her bed and haunts her
with the sound of its chalky fingers brushing against its
chalky skull.

With all the mystery with which these men and women
are surrounded, there is never any violation of character.
Their feelings are recognized; their actions, understood.

However well Frost portrays Yankee men and women,
he would scarcely be the poet of New England if he did
not love the New England country, if he did not write
of its trees, and fields, its birds, and flowers. In almost
any poem that one may choose, there can be discovered
some telling phrase descriptive of the things about him.
Titles of poems suggest Frost's close interest in and knowledge of country life: "A Hillside Thaw," "Gathering
Leaves," "Evening in a Sugar Orchard," "Pea Brush,"
"The Cow in Apple Time." The full flavor of his country
love is suggested in "Runaway" or in "Good-Bye and
Keep Cold."

GOOD-BYE AND KEEP COLD

This saying good-bye on the edge of the dark
And cold to an orchard so young in the bark
Reminds me of all that can happen to harm
An orchard away at the end of the farm
All winter, cut off by a hill from the house.
I don't want it girdled by rabbit and mouse,
I don't want it dreamily nibbled for browse
By deer, and I don't want it budded by grouse.

(If certain it wouldn't be idle to call
I'd summon grouse, rabbit, and deer to the wall
And warn them away with a stick for a gun.) .
I don't want it stirred by the heat of the sun.
(We made it secure against being, I hope,
By setting it out on a northerly slope.)
No orchard's the worse for the wintriest storm;
But one thing about it, it mustn't get warm.
"How often already you've had to be told,
Keep cold, young orchard. Good-bye and keep cold.
Dread fifty above more than fifty below."
I have to be gone for a season or so.
My business awhile is with different trees,
Less carefully nourished, less fruitful than these,
And such as is done to their wood with an axe—
Maples and birches and tamaracks.
I wish I could promise to lie in the night
And think of an orchard's arboreal plight
When slowly (and nobody comes with a light)
Its heart sinks lower under the sod.
But something has to be left to God.

This knowledge of things and of people is not the knowledge of the casual visitor who stands at a distance, looks about him at things not entirely familiar to him, and then murmurs "How quaint." It is the knowledge that comes from intimate contact with men, that has its basis in life and work shared with the people of whom he writes. This understanding through labor is a definite theme of

Frost's philosophy. An early poem, the one that won him his first school appointment, "The Tuft of Flowers," expresses it:

> "Men work together," I told him from the heart,
> "Whether they work together or apart."

The idea is further developed in "Mending Wall." What brings men together is good; what separates them is bad.

> Before I built a wall I'd ask to know
> What I was walling in or out,
> And to whom I was like to give offense.

The speaker in "Mending Wall" could suggest to his neighbor various reasons why the wall should not be built. He might say that the "elves" wanted it down;

> But it's not elves exactly, and I'd rather
> He said it for himself.

Man, Frost would say, must express his thoughts for himself; he must do his own thinking and act his own deeds. But he can do neither unless he is able and willing to face reality. It is this ability, this power to see things as they are that saves Frost from pessimism. It is this that makes him not so much a romantic or a religious poet as a naturalistic one. One must face the facts.

This acceptance of things as they are is suggested by the courage with which he faces the questionings of *West-*

Running Brook, and is very definitely expressed in "The Armful":

THE ARMFUL

For every parcel I stoop down to seize,
I lose some other off my arms and knees,
And the whole pile is slipping, bottles, buns,
Extremes too hard to comprehend at once,
Yet nothing one would like to leave behind.
With all I have to hold with, hand and mind
And heart, if need be, I will do my best
To keep their building balanced at my breast.
I crouch down to prevent them as they fall;
Then sit down in the middle of them all.
I had to drop the armful in the road
And try to stack them in a better load.

This is the crux of poetry of observation—the poetry of sight. But Frost has been called "the poet of sight and insight." And so, as in "The Armful," or as in "Mending Wall," one must look beneath the surface statement for the poem's inner meaning. Most of his poems should be read with this in mind: the poet from some observation of ordinary things or from some usual occurrence draws a fundamental and general truth. In "Wild Grapes," for example, the little girl whose weight was not sufficient to hold down the branches of the tree crowned with the grapes she was gathering, who was swung up high into the air, and who was afraid to let go her hold and drop, reflects later as a grown woman:

I had not taken the first step in knowledge;
I had not learned to let go with the hands,
As still I have not learned to with the heart,
And have no wish to with the heart—nor need,
That I can see.

Again, in "Birches," that delicate poem about the pliant
trees, there are both a surface picture and a deeper truth.

BIRCHES

When I see birches bend to left and right
Across the lines of straighter darker trees,
I like to think some boy's been swinging them.
But swinging doesn't bend them down to stay.
Ice-storms do that. Often you must have seen them
Loaded with ice a sunny winter morning
After a rain. They click upon themselves
As the breeze rises, and turn many-colored
As the stir cracks and crazes their enamel.
Soon the sun's warmth makes them shed crystal shells
Shattering and avalanching on the snow-crust—
Such heaps of broken glass to sweep away
You'd think the inner dome of heaven had fallen.
They are dragged to the withered bracken by the load,
And they seem not to break: though once they are bowed
So low for long, they never right themselves:
You may see their trunks arching in the woods
Years afterwards, trailing their leaves on the ground,
Like girls on hands and knees that throw their hair

Before them over their heads to dry in the sun.
But I was going to say when Truth broke in
With all her matter-of-fact about the ice-storm
I should prefer to have some boy bend them
As he went out and in to fetch the cows—
Some boy too far from town to learn baseball,
Whose only play was what he found himself,
Summer or winter, and could play alone.
One by one he subdued his father's trees
By riding them down over and over again
Until he took the stiffness out of them,
And not one but hung limp, not one was left
For him to conquer. He learned all there was
To learn about not launching out too soon
And so not carrying the tree away
Clear to the ground. He always kept his poise
To the top branches, climbing carefully
With the same pains you use to fill a cup
Up to the brim, and even above the brim.
Then he flung outward, feet first, with a swish,
Kicking his way down through the air to the ground.
So was I once myself a swinger of birches.
And so I dream of going back to be.
It's when I'm weary of considerations,
And life is too much like a pathless wood
Where your face burns and tickles with the cobwebs
Broken across it, and one eye is weeping
From a twig's having lashed across it open.
I'd like to get away from earth awhile

And then come back to it and begin over.
May no fate willfully misunderstand me
And half grant what I wish and snatch me away
Not to return. Earth's the right place for love:
I don't know where it's likely to go better.
I'd like to go by climbing a birch tree,
And climb black branches up a snow-white trunk
Toward heaven, till the tree could bear no more,
But dipped its top and set me down again.
That would be good both going and coming back.
One could do worse than be a swinger of birches.

The truth that Frost discovers he does not preach. Nor does he sing it as would a lyric poet interested chiefly in self-expression. He talks it over as a neighbor with neighbors. He does not force it upon his reader. Rather, he invites him to share it. This friendly attitude, this kindly invitation to share his life and song, is the keynote to all his poetry.

THE PASTURE

I'm going out to clean the pasture spring;
I'll only stop to rake the leaves away
(And wait to watch the water clear, I may):
I sha'n't be gone long.—You come too.

I'm going out to fetch the little calf
That's standing by the mother. It's so young,
It totters when she licks it with her tongue.
I sha'n't be gone long.—You come too.

POETICAL WORKS

A BOY'S WILL	*Henry Holt and Co.*
NORTH OF BOSTON	*Henry Holt and Co.*
MOUNTAIN INTERVAL	*Henry Holt and Co.*
SELECTED POEMS	*Henry Holt and Co.*
NEW HAMPSHIRE	*Henry Holt and Co.*
WEST-RUNNING BROOK	*Henry Holt and Co.*

AMY LOWELL

AMY LOWELL

DESPITE her traducers, there's always a heart
Hid away in her poems for the seeking; impas-
sioned,
Beneath silver surfaces cunningly fashioned
To baffle coarse pryings, it waits for the touch
Of a man who takes surfaces only as such. . . .
  .   .   .   .
Her books follow each other despite all the riot,
For, oddly enough, there's a queer, crumpled quiet
Perpetually round her, a crazy-quilt tent
Blinding her happily from the event.
Armed to the teeth like an old Samurai,
Juggling with jewels like the ancient genii,
Hung all over with mouse-traps of meters, and cages
Of bright-plumaged rhythms, with pages and pages
Of colours slit up into streaming confetti
Which give the appearance of something sunsetty
And gorgeous, and flowing—a curious sight
She makes in her progress, a modern White Knight,
Forever explaining her latest inventions
And assuring herself of all wandering attentions
By pausing at times to sing, in a duly
Appreciative manner an aria from Lully.

In these lines from *A Critical Fable,* Amy Lowell
draws her own portrait. With characteristic vividness she
suggests her love of color, of music, and of beautiful and
curious objects—all elements of her poetry; she calls
attention to her own experiments in verse form and her
efforts to explain them to a critical, and frequently hostile,
public; and in her phrase "queer crumpled quiet," she
gives an indication of the meaning that literature and her
own poems had for her. For her heart, which she declares
hidden in her poetry and which she bids one seek beneath
the silver surfaces, must appear a heart beset by conflicts:
the conflict between Puritan tradition and conservatism and
radical independence of thought and of action; that between New England coldness and an oriental love of
warmth and beauty; the one between exquisite thoughts
and desires and a large unattractive body; or, to use appropriate symbols, the constant contrast between huge strong
black cigars and delicate Japanese prints. The solution to
this opposition lay not so much in struggle as in with-
drawal; and so, although she was a modern, alert to and
in sympathy with the twentieth century, Amy Lowell
found her greatest joy in the spirit of an earlier age and
sought in the world of literature a retreat from the world
about her.

The family tradition behind Amy Lowell pointed un-
mistakably to a life of literary and social interests. The
first American Lowell, one Percival Lowle, a merchant
from Bristol, Somersetshire, arrived in Newburyport,
Massachusetts, in the second quarter of the seventeenth

AMY LOWELL

century. He is the author of a poem written on the death of Governor Winthrop:

> Here you have Lowell's loyalty
> Penned with slender skill
> And with it no good poetry,
> But certainly good will.

One of Percival's descendants, John Lowell, was a member of the Continental Congress. John's son Charles was the father of the poet James Russell Lowell; another son, Francis Cabot, for whom Lowell, Massachusetts, was named, became the founder of the cotton industry in the United States. An older son, John, Amy's great-grandfather, was a lawyer who won local literary fame by newspaper articles signed "The Boston Rebel" and "The Norfolk Farmer." He was known, too, for his greenhouses in Roxbury, Massachusetts. His son, John Amory Lowell, manifested the same kinds of interests; he was the first trustee of Lowell Institute and at Bromley Vale established noted gardens. Augustus Lowell, Amy's father, carried on the family tradition, becoming, in his turn, the head of the Institute and developing the gardens at his home, Sevenels, in Brookline.

On her mother's side, Amy Lowell's ancestry was no less distinguished. Her maternal grandfather, Abbott Lawrence, was at one time minister to England. Her own mother, Katherine Bigelow Lawrence, possessed many accomplishments; not only was she a skilled musician who could sing and play three instruments, but she was also an able linguist with five languages at her command.

The children who by "right of long inheritance" enjoyed these standards of culture and of achievement were Percival, who as a noted astronomer was to chart the canals on Mars; Abbott Lawrence, who was to become the third Lowell in direct descent who headed Lowell Institute and the president of Harvard University; and Amy, born February 9, 1874.

The little girl received her education through private tutoring and through the liberating effects of travel. Her mother was her real teacher, from whom she derived her thorough knowledge of French and her interest in music. From her father she inherited a love of flowers. And from an extended European trip, taken when she was eight years old, must have come the color and light of strange places that were to brighten her poems.

In fact, these elements of childhood developed into lifelong interests and were to enter again and again into her poetry. Her love of music shows itself in the imagery she frequently chooses; in reference to old compositions—

> At once she went
> And tinkled airs from Lully's *Carnival*
> And *Bacchus* newly brought from France—

or in a knowledge of musical form, which is the structural basis of such poems as "The Cremona Violin."

So far as her garden love is concerned, one finds it throughout her verses, which are gay with the bright color of flowers. Almost any poem chosen at random will give a quick impression of a flower, a vivid image of "hooded gentians" and "hardy sumachs." Many will sug-

gest a more detailed but always tender study of a flower's
beauty:

The ladies,
Wistaria Blossom, Cloth-of-Silk, and Deep Snow,
With their ten attendants,
Are come to Asakusa
To gaze at peonies,
To admire crimson-carmine peonies,
To stare in admiration at bomb-shaped, white and sulphur
     peonies,
To caress with a soft finger
Single, rose-flat peonies,
Tight, incurved, red-edged peonies,
Spin-wheel circle, amaranth peonies.

The technique of garden planning and care, which she
mastered for the sake of her own gardens at Sevenels,
becomes the theme of an entire poem, as in "Planning the
Garden":

> Bring pencils, fine-pointed,
> For our writing must be infinitesimal;
> And bring sheets of paper
> To spread before us. . . .
>
> There, it is done;
> Seal up the paper.
> Let us go to bed and dream of flowers.

It was at Sevenels that Amy Lowell was born. Here
she spent her childhood. And here, in a manner not fre-

quently encountered in changing America, she was to make her permanent home until her death. Sevenels, an estate of about ten acres, five miles from the center of Boston, had been developed from a farm into a country estate by Stephen Higginson, a member of the Continental Congress. It changed hands several times before it was bought by Amy Lowell's father in 1867. "Some one built an ugly but substantial brick house," she writes, "which, if pleasant to live in, adds nothing to the charm of the gardens." The old-fashioned gardens were bordered by groves of trees which gave the impression of being real woods. Beyond lay meadows for mowing, thick growths of trees, and, encircling it all, a wall that protected the little domain from the outside world.

One can imagine the active life that went on behind those walls! Amy's energy expressed itself in tennis, in playing with the animals on the place, in riding. She herself tells of her childhood games: "And many are the Indians I have shot when out scouting with my bow and arrows as they peered for a moment from behind a distant tree-trunk, and, in spite of a little confusion in my mind as to whether I was Robin Hood or the Last of the Mohicans, I delight to record I never missed my man."

There are references to childhood in several of her poems. However much the views expressed may have been modified by poetic demands, one feels that they must have had some basis in reality or in desire. So one can find suggestions of the active life of the child in "Climbing": "High in the apple tree climbing I go"; of

the more contemplative and imaginative life in "A Fairy
Tale":

> On winter nights beside the nursery fire
> We read the fairy tale, while glowing coals
> Builded its pictures.

and in "The Pleiades," in which the stars are thought
to be the toys of some "nice little angel boy":

> I wish he'd come and play with me.
> We'd have such fun, for it would be
> A most unusual thing for boys
> To feel that they had stars for toys.

What is significant in this material of memory, in
"Sea Shell," for example, and in "Crescent Moon," is
that the interests are those of a boy ever so much more
than they are those of a girl. As a child, it would seem,
the poet was already withdrawing from actuality into a
world of Otherwise.

But disappointment frequently attended these efforts
to escape. This note of failure, of incompletion, is struck
in the previously mentioned "A Fairy Tale":

But always there was one unbidden guest
Who cursed the child and left it bitterness.

The fire falls asunder, and all is changed,
I am no more a child, and what I see
Is not a fairy tale, but life, my life.
The gifts are there, the many pleasant things:
Health, wealth, long-settled friendships with a name

Which honors all who bear it, and the power
Of making words obedient. This is much;
But overshadowing all is still the curse,
That never shall I be fulfilled by love!

These were not moods and attitudes to be lightly
shaken off. Throughout the great mass of her poetry,
one finds the poet's efforts to create a world more satisfactory than the real world she knew. She writes frequently with the point of view of a man. She creates vague,
ephemeral ideals which, too often, are elusive. She realizes
that her desires will not be fulfilled, and her remedy is—
more dreams!

But life at Sevenels was not in itself a life of bitterness. In spite of a mother who was an invalid and of a
father who held stern convictions about the conventions
of conduct, there were gay times in the substantial home.
Elizabeth Ward Perkins,[1] a friend of the poet, tells of
a visit she paid at Sevenels when Amy was eighteen. She
writes of the parties at Papanti's, the local dancing-
master's ballroom; she tells of the books the two girls
read, of the verses they wrote, of the criticism they gave
each other. She describes the life of Amy and her family:

"At eighteen it was exhilirating to watch Amy outdoors with horses and dogs, in gardens with flowers and
flowering shrubs, moon-gazing from the roof of Sevenels,
or in the woods near by; to watch her indoors with books,
and still more books—walls, tables, and chairs laden with
books—with well-tempered pencils and docile pens. . . .

[1] "Amy Lowell of New England," *Scribner's*, September 1927.

"All the children a dozen years older than her friend Amy, married and unmarried, were at home; the men, authorities already in government and astronomy, the women, keen for civic betterment and public affairs, with young children in their nurseries. As they gathered for the over-abundant meals of the era, it seemed to the stranger quite possible that the art of listening might be dispensed with, having become superfluous. Any two members of this family could talk and listen simultaneously, effecting a great economy in time and patience, for conflicting opinions might be stated, registered, and answered at the same moment. New England reserve did not prevail at the large table."

In 1895 there came a break in the family circle, with the death of Mrs. Lowell. During the next few years, the daughter traveled. There was a winter spent on the Nile, another at a fruit ranch in El Cajon, California; a summer spent in Europe. In 1900 the father died. Amy purchased the family home and became closely identified with it and with the educational life of the town.

Always she had been motivated by a vague desire to write. At thirteen she had written some verses and had formulated a mild ambition to become a writer of stories. It was not, however, until 1902, at the age of twenty-eight, that she arrived at the definite determination to become a poet. Then, with characteristic energy, she gave herself up to a close study of the art. The craft of poetry, she felt, could and must be learned. The preface to *Sword Blades and Poppy Seed* explains her attitude: "As a matter of fact, the poet must learn his trade, in the same

manner and with the same painstaking care, as the cabinet-
maker." For eight years, dividing her time between
Brookline and Dublin, New Hampshire, she applied herself closely to study. She was her only critic, and a severe
one. Finally in the *Atlantic Monthly* for August 1910
appeared her first printed poem, a sonnet called "A Fixed
Idea."

In 1912 was published *A Dome of Many-Coloured
Glass*, a book, which, in spite of the classic form in which
many of its poems were cast, hinted at experiments in a
different manner, in a freer method which was to become
the "new poetry."

In 1913, on a visit to England, Amy Lowell met Ezra
Pound, the leader of a group of young poets, the Imagists.
She was drawn to this group and found that their tenets
were such as she had formulated for herself. She joined
forces with them and was represented in *Des Imagistes*,
a collection of poetry appearing in 1914. But the original
band shortly broke up. Miss Lowell became the nucleus
of a new group composed of Richard Aldington, H. D.
(Hilda Doolittle), F. S. Flint, D. H. Lawrence, and John
Gould Fletcher. For three successive years she directed
the publication of the anthologies of their poems, *Some
Imagist Poets*.

The ensuing years were spent in the expounding of the
literary beliefs of the new poetry; in critical writing; in
lectures, particularly a series in 1915 at Boston, New
York, and Chicago, and one in 1917-18 at the Brooklyn
Institute of Arts and Sciences; and in the creation of her
own verse. With fair regularity her books appeared; in

1914, *Sword Blades and Poppy Seeds*; 1915, *Six French Poets*, a critical study of those to whom she owed much; 1916, *Men, Women, and Ghosts*; 1917, *Tendencies in Modern American Poetry*, the first clear-cut presentation of the new poetry; 1918, *Can Grande's Castle*; 1919, *Pictures of the Floating World*; 1921, *Legends* and *Fir-Flower Tablets*, the latter in collaboration with Florence Ayscough; 1922, *A Critical Fable*, a rhymed satire on the modern poets, modeled on James Russell Lowell's *A Fable for Critics*, published anonymously, and acknowledged by its author two years later; 1925, the monumental biography, *John Keats*, and *What's O'clock*, on the proofs of which the poet had just finished working when she died.

It was in her critical writing rather than in her own verse that Amy Lowell showed herself the bold fighter and leader of a cause. True, much of her poetry, because of its then unusual manner, aroused hostile criticism; but it was accepted and acclaimed by enough people to bring to its author acknowledged honors. Twice she was chosen Phi Beta Kappa poet, by Tufts in 1918 and by Columbia in 1920. In the latter year she received the honorary degree of Litt.D. from Baylor University, and in 1921 she was the Francis Bergen Foundation lecturer at Yale and the Marshall Woods lecturer at Brown.

It was during this period, when books were being written and academic honors received, that those qualities in Amy Lowell were emphasized which made her a great celebrity and almost a legendary figure. She became known for her stalwart independence of spirit. The de-

fiance with which she overthrew literary conventions was
duplicated by her defiance of the social demands of conservative Boston. Her critics she met with courage. Val-
iantly she fought for the right of the individual to express himself as he preferred. At times bitterness crept
into her attacks and counter-attacks, impatience at those
who could not see the right as she saw it or who would
not submissively yield to her domineering personality.

The force of that personality could not be concealed;
her mannerisms and habits came to be part of the general
fund of common information. The public were made
familiar with her idiosyncrasies; the big black cigars, the
bed with its sixteen pillows, the mirrors in her New York
hotel which, on her arrival, had to be covered with black.

For always she was sensitive about her appearance.
Once when she was making an appointment with an artist,
she telephoned him: "I am a terrible-looking object. Do
you know anything about my appearance?" On his arrival
at her hotel he fell a victim to her personal magnetism.
"I am fat," was her response, "but not a fat-head."

What did she look like? She was exceedingly stout and
ungainly. She had a massive head, but a face with something almost childish and prim about it. As if to subject
her body to restraint, she wore plain dresses of rich dark
satin, with net undersleeves, and high stiff-boned collars.

This costume, worn almost like a uniform in spite of
changing modes, suggests her defensive indifference to
the styles and expectations of the world about her. With
a sublime superiority to what the world might expect of
life in the large mansard-roofed mansion, she spurned

the luxurious sleeping-rooms to choose for her own a room high up in the attic under the slate roof.

Elizabeth Shepley Sergeant, in her book *Fire Under the Andes*,[2] describes it:

"Here, too, kimonas and typewriters, secretaries, and—in their time—Scotch sheep dogs, maids and visitors, breakfasts and lunches, fires and electric fans, manuscripts and bandages, keen-pointed pencils and blunt-pointed cigars, could be mingled in that highly organized confusion and bustle which were the sphere of a poet's more executive hours. Her wide, low bedroom, opening off a wide low hall, and bursting with books like all the rest of the house, was the center of her kingdom, and her wide low bed was the very nucleus of this central cell; it had exactly sixteen pillows and was sunned and cooled by a couple of dormer windows overlooking the sunken gardens where, in summer, fireflies were sometimes seen to light their lamps along the round, clipped evergreens before she left it for a dinner late and ever later. I have seen her reading in that bed under a black umbrella in the bright light of mid-afternoon, smoking, of course, the equally black cigar; I have seen her 'making it'—as she did always with her own hands—at one A.M., the faithful Irish maid, whom she adored and abused, standing by to plump the pillows."

Could it have been the same gray-haired maid who was seen one morning crawling over the piazza roof so that she might pass Miss Lowell's room without disturb-

[2] *Fire Under the Andes: a Group of North American Portraits*, Knopf, New York.

ing her sleep? For Miss Lowell's hours for work and for rest were not the same as other people's. With a charming disregard for the clock, she turned night into day, beginning her work at the time when most people are soundly sleeping. She was never on time for appointments, frequently keeping people waiting for an hour or more.

But dinner guests at Sevenels, whatever their hostess's habits, must always be prompt. The guests would begin their dinner and then hear Miss Lowell's voice calling from her attic bedroom two long flights above. She would enter the dining-room followed by her seven dogs, two of whom, chosen for their good deportment, would accompany her later to the library fireplace.

Harriet Monroe, the editor of *Poetry*, in an article in the July 1925 issue of that magazine, gives a glimpse of that huge library and of Amy Lowell presiding in it:

"I remember with special delight the great library whither she used to descend before dinner-time from her private domain on the third floor. Here, after the stately repast, she would sit enthroned in the corner of the lounge, and here she loved to linger and talk until at least three o'clock in the morning—for she always inverted day and night and felt pathetically aggrieved if her visitor's spirit did not rise to her hours. She was an eager and delightful talker, indulging a discursive and experimental mind —a mind with much shrewdness and common sense and whimsical humor under its more decorative impulses. And in that richly rusty old beautiful room, book-filled to the ceiling, she seemed completely at home with the forebears of her blood who had lived there and of her intellect, whom she could invoke from her ten thousand volumes."

With energetic thoroughness, Miss Lowell attended to the management of her home. "I hate to plan and order meals," she declared, "but I do it every day and look after all of the details that devolve upon a housekeeper." One can be sure that no detail escaped, no detail from those of the furnace and basement to those of the beloved garden.

That her directions were properly executed one may also be sure. For Miss Lowell was an autocrat of the old school. Servants and friends were bound close to her by affection, but she was hurt if she could not order even the most intimate details of their lives. Editors and publishers had to submit to her. When she was in New York, she bade them call upon her and it was she who told them which poems they might print, not they who were permitted to choose—or reject!

When Harriet Monroe began *Poetry*, she accepted some of Miss Lowell's poems. These, however, had not been published before the two women met for the first time at a dinner in Chicago. The poet's acknowledgment of the introduction to the editor was, "Well, since you've taken 'em, why don't you print 'em?"

With this directness and force Miss Lowell attacked any problem. The town board of Brookline was considering a law prohibiting children from skating, sliding, or dragging sleds on sidewalks. Miss Lowell scathingly denounced it. "Are we going to make all our children crim-

inals? Are we to be entirely officialized? Are we to abandon entirely our constitutional rights to the pursuit of
happiness?" The law was amended.

While she was intolerant of stupidity, she was untir-
ing in her efforts to help those in whom she had faith.
With a strange diffidence she would suggest the correct
reading of her poems. "I don't read those lines that way.
Your way may be better than my way, of course!" Un-
sparingly, she gave her time to encouraging young poets
and to working over their verse.

Her energy and dynamic force kept her going in spite
of ill-health. An illness necessitating an operation was not
allowed to interfere with her work on the Keats biography. Finally that book was completed and a trip to
Europe planned.

On April 4, 1925, her friends gathered in Boston to
honor her with a farewell dinner. Asked for her favorite
poem, she read "Lilacs":

> Lilacs,
> False blue,
> White,
> Purple,
> Colour of lilac.
> Heart-leaves of lilac all over New England,
> Roots of lilac under all the soil of New England,
> Lilac in me because I am New England,
> Because my roots are in it,
> Because my leaves are of it,
> Because my flowers are for it,

Because it is my country,
And I speak to it of itself
And sing of it with my own voice
Since certainly it is mine.

This last stanza was read movingly and dramatically. But the poet's voice lacked its usual fire and ring.

Shortly after she was taken fatally sick. The European trip was canceled. On May 12 she died.

A year later, in May 1926, *What's O'clock* was awarded the Pulitzer Prize for poetry. And that the record of her books may be complete, it should be noted here that there have been two posthumous volumes of poetry: *East Wind* (1926) and *Ballads for Sale* (1927).

Miss Lowell's will bequeathed her valuable collection of books and manuscripts to Harvard. Her estate was left to Mrs. Ada Dwyer Russell, an actress, who since 1912 had been her constant companion. Finally, provision was made for the Amy Lowell Poetry Traveling Scholarship to give each year to some poet "of American birth" of "good standing or promise" $2,000 for a year's traveling, necessarily outside of North America.

Thus even beyond the term of her life she manifested her interest in poetry, for which she came to be the acknowledged spokesman. Her attitude toward the art is made clear in her two books of criticism, her articles and interviews, and in the prefaces to her own books of poems.

Poetry, for her, was one of the luxuries, the refinements of life. "I wish that no man could expect to make a living by writing," she declared in an interview with the poet, Joyce Kilmer.

The sole aim of poetry is the creation of beauty. This is maintained in the preface to *Sword Blades and Poppy Seed*: "In the first place, I wish to state my firm belief that poetry should not try to teach, that it should exist simply because it is a created beauty, even if sometimes the beauty of a Gothic grotesque."

This beauty can be found in the poetry of former times as well as in the poetry of the present. Yet, however keen was the consciousness of poetical tradition that Amy Lowell possessed, it was the "new poetry" that found in her a champion. It was the new poetry's terminology and purpose that she strove to elucidate. For her the new poetry was a matter of spirit rather than of form. But because form is more easily recognized than spirit, popular interest centered in her definitions of *vers libre* and of polyphonic prose, two forms which much of the new poetry assumed.

Vers libre is an old form newly named, "a verse form based upon cadence rather than upon exact meter." It is non-syllabic; the stress is one of chief accents only. It depends upon a sense of balance, a satisfactory rounding of groups of words; and it may be either rhymed or rhymeless.

Polyphonic prose was the creation originally of M. Paul Fort. There is a story that M. Fort, disturbed that a French magazine would pay for prose but insisted that publication itself was sufficient reward for poetry, met editorial requirements and his own needs by submitting his poetry in paragraphed form. Whatever truth there may be to the tale, polyphonic prose is prose only in typographical arrangement. It is a very flexible and elastic form; it employs the devices of conventional poetry, rhythm, rhyme, assonance, alliteration, and return. "Its only touchstone," says Miss Lowell, "is the taste and feeling of its author."

Finally, she formulated for popular understanding the tenets of Imagism, with which she identified her work. Imagism meant the abandonment of worn-out phrases, poetic diction, and tortured inversions; and the substitution of the language of common speech, the exact and not the merely decorative word. It permitted freedom in the choice of subject matter, a freedom limited, however, by standards of good taste. It insisted on the necessity of new rhythms to express new moods, and it urged still more emphatically concentrated, definite images in place of vague generalities.

To what extent does Amy Lowell's own poetry follow the principles which she expounded?

In *A Dome of Many-Coloured Glass*, one finds too many reminders of an old, creaking poetic method. There are trite phrases like "sacrificial urn" and "oaten pipe"; words distorted for rhyme or rhythm, as "employ" used for "employment"; awkward inversions, as

> Whirl round the earth as never sun
> Has his diurnal journey run

or such stereotyped and banal stanzas as this from "Petals":

Life is a stream
On which we strew
Petal by petal the flower of our heart.

If the objection is raised that these, all taken from her first book, are merely the errors of a beginner, errors which maturity was to avoid, one must admit that similar defects are found even in her later work. Accents are wrenched as in "stripéd" and "perfuméd." Words are misused or coined to meet poetic demands. "Vaunt," for example, becomes a noun; "strown" becomes the past participle of "strew"; "beautifulness" is simply invented and thrust on the reader. Word order may be completely upset as in

It told her that his wound,
The writer's, had so well recovered.

One wonders, too, how so stern a self-critic would permit such lines as the following to remain in her poetry:

And covered Clotilde and the angry snake,
He bit her, but what difference did that make!

Such negative criticism, however, is valueless. The isolation of flaws from the great mass of poetry, their intense scrutiny under the magnifying-glass, connotes little; and in this case, at all events, gives little conception of the vigor and beauty that are present.

Beyond all else, there are throughout the poems vivid, sharp-cut images and a lively feeling for color. Consider, for example, the wizardry of color in "The Captured Goddess":

> I followed her for long,
> With gazing eyes and stumbling feet.
> I cared not where she led me,
> My eyes were full of colours;
> Saffrons, rubies, the yellow of beryls,
> And the indigo-blue of quartz;
> Flights of rose, layers of chrysoprase,
> Points of orange, spirals of vermilion,
> The spotted gold of tiger-lily petals,
> The loud pink of bursting hydrangeas.
> I followed,
> And watched for the flashing of her wings.

Inevitably perfect are such figures as:

> The pointed, tulip-flame
> Of a tallow candle

and "a little wan and ravelled smile," "Carlotta's heart dropped beats like knitting-stitches," or the poem "Middle Age":

Like black ice
Scrolled over with unintelligible patterns by an ignorant
     skater
Is the dulled surface of my heart.

Was ever the wind more deftly personified than in these lines from "White Currants"?

Is it because the raucous wind is hurtling round the house-
    corners?
I see it with curled lips and stripped fangs, gaunt with a
    hunting energy,
Come to snout, and nibble, and kill the little crocus roots.

One of her most effective devices for presenting a vivid
picture is to describe impressions of one sense in terms
of another sense. Sound, for example, may be translated
into sight:

A spoon falls upon the floor with the impact of metal
    striking stone.
And the sound throws across the room
Sharp, invisible zigzags
Of silver.

The opening lines of "A Lady" illustrate this method
well:
            You are beautiful and faded
            Like an old opera tune
            Played upon a harpsichord;
            Or like the sun-flooded silks
            Of an eighteenth-century boudoir.

One can find in her poetry, too, excellent examples of
the so-called new forms of poetry. *Vers libre* may be employed by her for the sake of an effective, devastating last
line, as in "The Tree of Scarlet Berries," where, after
longing for the bright red berries, she says:

But, in the mist, I only scratched my hands on the thorns.
Probably, too, they are bitter.

Or it may be used because of the exact matching of
thought to rhythm. The best example of highly satisfactory *vers libre,* and one of the best of Amy Lowell's
poems as well as one of her favorites, is "Patterns":

> I walk down the garden-paths,
> And all the daffodils
> Are blowing, and the bright blue squills.
> I walk down the patterned garden-paths
> In my stiff, brocaded gown.
> With my powdered hair and jewelled fan,
> I too am a rare
> Pattern. As I wander down
> The garden-paths.

The lady has received a letter announcing her lover's
death in battle. But she restrains her overwhelming grief
and bravely conceals it, for she realizes that life must
continue in the pattern set for it:

In Summer and in Winter I shall walk
Up and down
The patterned garden-paths
In my stiff, brocaded gown.
The squills and daffodils
Will give place to pillared roses, and to asters and to snow.
I shall go
Up and down
In my gown

Gorgeously arrayed,
Boned and stayed.
And the softness of my body will be guarded from
    embrace
By each button, hook, and lace.
For the man who should loose me is dead,
Fighting with the Duke in Flanders,
In a pattern called a war.
Christ! what are patterns for?

Just as there is a pattern for the lady's life, so is there
a pattern for the poem. Blue and yellow, pink and silver,
the brocaded gown, the phrase "I shall walk up and
down" repeated in variety, take the place of conventional
rhythm and verse form.

Miss Lowell's experiments in metrics are numerous.
In "A Cremona Violin," for example, she uses movement
in poetry as a musician uses movement in music. In "A
Roxbury Garden" she modifies her experiment; here it is
the movement of hoops and of battledores and shuttle-
cocks that is suggested.

The poems making up the "Towns in Colour" section
of *Men, Women and Ghosts* illustrate what their author
calls the "unrelated method." This consists of the cata-
loguing of details for the purpose of building up a definite
impression. "Thompson's Lunch Room" and "An Opera
House" are excellent illustrations of this method, the one
a study in white, the other a study in gold. "Red Slippers"
in the same group of poems is possibly the best-known
example of her polyphonic prose. But there are equally

effective passages, this from "Malmaison," for example:
"Night. The Empress sits alone, and the clock ticks,
one after one. The clock nicks off edges of her life. She
is chipped like an old bit of china, she is frayed like a
garment of last year's wearing. She is soft, crinkled, like
a fading rose. And each minute flows by brushing against
her, shearing off another and another petal. The Empress
crushes her breasts with her hands and weeps. And the
tall clouds sail over Malmaison like a procession of stately
ships bound for the moon."

The world which is described in Miss Lowell's poetry
is, for the most part, a world of little things, of the
objects around her, in which she delighted. It is a man-
made world, a world of landscaped gardens, a world of
the cities of man, a world in which a "Rag Picker" and
"Thompson's Lunch Room" can find place.

Of necessity, then, there is a sense of character. This
may express itself in the delicately satiric sketches of
"Gouache Pictures of Italy" in *Ballads For Sale*, or in
the moving, tragic figures of "The Overgrown Pasture"
in *Men, Women and Ghosts* and in *East Wind*. "The
Overgrown Pasture" has running through it a motif of
loneliness and maladjustment which comes to a poignant
climax in "Number 3 On the Docket." A woman, grief-
stricken by her son's death and maddened by the unbroken silence of the farm, kills her husband:

> I had to break a way out somehow,
> Somethin' was closin' in
> An' I was stiflin'.

Ed's loggin' axe was there,
An' I took it.

In *East Wind*, a collection of New England stories, the author's sympathy with the loneliness of life is shown again and again, but particularly in "The Doll" and in "The Day That Was That Day."

Her characters are presented with narrative skill. "The Great Adventure of Max Breuck," for example, tells a complicated story, which, for the handling of plot, may well be compared with the intensely compressed story of "Clear, with Light Variable Winds." There are other stories in *Legends*, a collection of eleven tales of different backgrounds, "bits of fact, or guesses at fact, pressed into the form of a story and flung out into the world as markers of how much ground has been travelled." These tales, told in a variety of meters and forms, range from "A Legend of Porcelain" to "Many Swans," a sun myth of the North American Indians, and the bizarre European tale of "The Statue in the Garden."

Great though the poet's narrative skill is, it is always the characters and backgrounds rather than the incidents of plot that seem important. This is especially true of the panoramic pictures of history that she presents: "Sea Blue and Blood Red," the story of Nelson; "Guns as Keys; and the Great Gate Swings," the story of Commodore Perry's entrance into Japan, with an emphatic contrast of Western and Eastern civilization; and "The Bronze Horses," the majestic and overpowering sweep

of history as epitomized by the horses of St. Mark's.
"The Hammers" is a particularly effective poem of the
Napoleonic era. It sings the song of the hammers, those
that built Nelson's ships, those that pulled down the street
signs in Paris, those that, after the Austrian victory,
chipped the inscription on the Arc du Carrousel, those
that shod the horses of the army, and finally those that
built Napoleon's coffin.

In this sense of the past, Miss Lowell finds her refuge
from the present. The tragedy of the great war, in particular, drives her back into history. Although in "The
Bombardment" she gives a complete and moving picture of the modern destruction of a town, the war serves
as immediate subject for but few of her poems. It is
not that the war had no effect on her. In the preface to
Men, Women and Ghosts she declares that it cannot help
affect any one writing at the time, but "we are too near
it to do more than touch upon it." Again in *Can Grande's
Castle* she writes, "Yet today can never be adequately
expressed, largely because we are a part of it and only
a part."

If the past offered one avenue of escape from the
difficulties of adjustment to the present, irony offered
another. This irony may vary in intensity from that of
"The Precinct . . . Rochester," wherein the Dean is
strongly contrasted with those outside the Cathedral
Close "who care more for bread than for beauty," to that
of "Astigmatism," with Ezra Pound, the poet, spurning
all flowers because they are not roses, or of "La Ronde

du Diable," in which the poets' envy of each other is
satirized:

> Do we want laurels for ourselves most,
> Or most that no one else shall have any?

Yet, when she wills, Miss Lowell can be tender, as she
is in "Nuit Blanche" or in "Madonna of the Evening
Flowers":

> Then I see you,
> Standing under a spire of pale blue larkspur,
> With a basket of roses on your arm.
> You are cool, like silver,
> And you smile.
> I think the Canterbury bells are playing little tunes.

Bitterness, tenderness, whatever the grace-note may be,
the fundamental tone of Miss Lowell's poetry is that
of disappointment seeking relief in dreams, the pursuit
of some intangible, elusive ideal. It is sounded in "The
Starling" in her first book of poems:

> I weary for desires never guessed,
> For alien passions, strange imaginings
> To be some other person for a day.

It is heard again in "Behind Time" in *Ballads for Sale*,
one of her posthumously published volumes:

> So I sit
> Considering time and hating it.

It was only when death came that Amy Lowell was able to shake off the binding restraints of time. Some premonition of that final release must have come to her; it is suggested in "Rode the Six Hundred":

A June-bug has just flown in through my window,
And today I sat among narcissus and grape-hyacinths
Drinking the sudden sun.
The terrible Winter has passed
Flinging my garden full of flowers.
But for me I think it will not be long,
Not long,
Before it is the end.

Ah! my flowers!

Inheritance, New England tradition, demanded from Amy Lowell a fixed conduct of life: "The law exacts obedience. Instruct, I will conform." But the strength of her individuality was too great to be anything but independent. The conflict between the two forces drove the poet within herself and caused her to create an ideal world of dreams, to escape from the present into the peace of the past.

Her solution was purely a personal one. Of those other writers who are adjusted to the present she was an ardent champion; for them she demanded the right to free themselves of a strangling past and to express themselves as moderns. That they might avoid some of the pathos of her own life she exerted every effort of a powerful personality.

POETICAL WORKS

A DOME OF MANY-COLOURED GLASS
Houghton Mifflin Co.

SWORD BLADES AND POPPY SEEDS
Houghton Mifflin Co.

MEN, WOMEN AND GHOSTS   *Houghton Mifflin Co.*

CAN GRANDE'S CASTLE   *The Macmillan Company*

PICTURES OF THE FLOATING WORLD
The Macmillan Company

LEGENDS   *Houghton Mifflin Co.*

FIR-FLOWER TABLETS (in collaboration)
Houghton Mifflin Co.

A CRITICAL FABLE   *Houghton Mifflin Co.*

WHAT'S O'CLOCK   *Houghton Mifflin Co.*

EAST WIND   *Houghton Mifflin Co.*

BALLADS FOR SALE   *Houghton Mifflin Co.*

SELECTED POEMS   *Houghton Mifflin Co.*

EDNA ST. VINCENT MILLAY

EDNA ST. VINCENT MILLAY

A T ONE of her many appearances on the lecture
platform Edna St. Vincent Millay made a statement which serves to indicate the importance of poetry
in her own life. "Never stop reading poetry," she said,
"never stop reading poetry because of anything at all."
For her, poetry must be the accompaniment to life, not
—and this is significant—its substitute. Her own poetry
is intensely personal; yet it is not the poetry of seclusion
and of escape. It is the poetry of a full life, a life of
friends, college, acting, travel, and marriage. The poet
plays a part in the real world. She studies it as well as
herself. She finds wrongs and she finds sorrow. But she
finds beauty, too; and of this beauty she weaves her
songs.

The first beauties of which she must have been aware
were those of the Maine seacoast. There, in Rockland,
she was born on February 22, 1892, the daughter of
Henry Tolman and Cora M. Buzzelle Millay. In Rockland, and later in Camden, she lived a tomboy's life,
knowing intimately the wild stretches of wave and sand.
The beauty of the sea and her great love for it form a
haunting refrain to her poems. It is for the sea that she

longs whether she is in the city or whether she is on her inland farm in her "house on upland acres."

While she was enjoying the life of an active young girl, while she was attending the Camden public schools, she was writing poetry, encouraged in her efforts by her mother, a kindly, tolerant, and vivid personality. Indeed it would have been strange if, with so poetic and rhythmical a name, she had not felt herself something of a poet. But for the sake of accuracy it must be recorded that her first poems were signed not with her full name, but with the less melodious "E. Vincent Millay."

These early poems are to be found in the files of *St. Nicholas*, in those delightful back pages of the League where eager young contributors entered poems, stories, drawings, and photographs in monthly competitions. Time and again during 1908 and 1909, Edna sent poems to the magazine and saw them printed. For them she was made an honor member of the League; she received the League's silver medal and its gold medal. For the April 1908 number she wrote a poem called "Life." Life, she declares, is an imitation; so, she argues, with a youthful moral air, each one should live so that his life may be thought worthy of further imitation.

In the November issue for the same year is a delicate lyric called "Day's Rest-time." In contrast with this is another early poem, a jesting parody called "Young Mother Hubbard," in which a very frivolous version of the nursery-tale heroine discovers that the steak for her French poodle is too rare. She is so upset by this mishap that she faints away and needs a doctor's care. As for the poodle—he consumes all the meat and lies contentedly asleep.

It was for her poem called "Friends," in the May 1910 number, that the poet was awarded the League's highest honor: "As its young author has already won both a gold and a silver badge, and, therefore, is an honor member of the League, we gladly award a Cash Prize to the clever rhyme." It consists of the contrasted musings of a boy and a girl, the boy unable to understand the girl's fondness for sewing, the girl equally perplexed by the boy's interest in football. The characters are clearly presented. The lines run smoothly, and there is a nimble and somewhat complicated rhyming scheme.

Without exaggerating the importance of these poems, one may find in them several of the elements which characterize Miss Millay's later verse. There is, to begin with, an easy flow of words, a nice fitting of thought and meter that suggests the simple strength of her most successful lyrics. The imagery is delicate and beautiful. Besides these suggestions of method and technique, there are indications of the kinds of verse the poet was to produce. Is it too much to see in the Mother Hubbard parody a satiric vein that was to be most marked in some of the poems of *A Few Figs from Thistles*, or in the contrasted and clearly presented characterizations of "Friends" a power of character drawing and a dramatic sense that were to lead to the writing of plays culminating in *The King's Henchman*?

However apparent these qualities may now appear, they were at the time scarcely sufficient to prepare the public for an important literary event of 1912. In that year was published *The Lyric Year*, a collection of verse chosen from ten thousand poems by nearly two thousand writers. By a system of point awards, first prize went to a poem called "Second Avenue," by Orrick Jones, and second prizes to "To a Thrush" by Thomas Augustine Daly and "An Ode for the Centenary of the Birth of Robert Browning" by George Sterling. One of the judges, Ferdinand Earle, the editor of the volume, had found his choice for first award overruled. He had selected "Renascence," by Edna St. Vincent Millay. But though it did not win a prize, it received wide critical approval and was acclaimed as the book's outstanding poem.

It had been written in 1911, when the poet was but nineteen. It is because of its combination of a youthful simplicity of manner with a mature depth of feeling, a specific interest in objects with a mystic awareness of the essential unity of the universe, vivid objective pictures with a revelation of the poet's soul, that it is so remarkable.

The poem is written with a lyrical intensity and control that is unusual in so young a writer. That she was still young and a very real young person is suggested by a story that is told of her at this time. A poet, it is said, wrote her a rather solemn congratulatory letter on her achievement. To his surprise he received in answer a very frivolous letter filled with exuberance over the purchase of a pair of red dancing-slippers!

In 1913 this very real person entered Vassar College. Here "Vincent" took a large number of Latin courses, made warm friendships, and was keenly interested in dramatics. In her sophomore year, for example, she played the part ᴏ Eugene Marchbanks in Shaw's *Candida.* Of her performance the college paper, *The Vassar Miscellany,* writes: "The audience never lost a sense of Marchbanks' personality as a whole, its weakness, its strength, its lack of common sense and its grasp of the values of life. Every expression and gesture of his was full of restraint and exact appropriateness. From first to last he dominated the stage."

In play-writing, too, this interest manifested itself. Two of her plays were produced at college, *The Princess Marries the Page* and *Two Slatterns and a King.* The latter is a slight "moral interlude" on· the subject of chance, "that cunning infidel." The King seeks a bride, using· as a test the neatness of the maiden's kitchen. But, as chance would have it, Tidy's kitchen is upset by a train of untoward incidents, and Slut's, by a chance whim, is scrubbed and set in order. The King, deceived by its chance appearance, weds Slut—to his everlasting sorrow!

Another play, *The Wall of Dominoes,* was printed in *The Miscellany* and was Vassar's play entry in the literary competition of the Northern College Magazines. The college magazine published several poems by Miss Millay. "Interim," a somewhat long-drawn-out poem on death, won the prize in *The Miscellany* contest for 1914 and was later included in the *Vassar Book of Verse;* and "The Suicide," in the April 1916 issue of the magazine, a moral denunciation of the cowardice of suicide, was the Vassar entry in an intercollegiate competition.

1917 marked the end of her college years and the pub-

lication of her first book, *Renascence and Other Poems.*
This was most enthusiastically received. Harriet Monroe
in her review of it in *Poetry* said, "One would have to
go back a long way in literary history to find a young lyric
poet singing so freely and musically in such a big world.
Almost we hear a thrush at dawn, discovering the everlasting splendor of the morning."

The book reprinted the three earlier poems, "Interim,"
"The Suicide," and "Renascence." Something of the rapture of the last-named poem was repeated in "God's
World." This rapture, this thrilling at the beauty of this
world—

> What is the need of Heaven
> When earth can be so sweet?—

gives the book a tinge of mysticism; at the same time
there is a preoccupation with death and grief. "Interim,"
"The Suicide," "The Shroud," to name but a few poems,
show how much the poet's mind must have dwelt on the
transitoriness of life and of beauty.

But if she cannot reconcile herself to the thought of
the loss of beauty, she is not here rebellious. The restraint
both in feeling and in manner is perhaps nowhere better
expressed than in the five unnamed sonnets, of which the
last may serve as an example:

> If I should learn, in some quite casual way,
>   That you were gone, not to return again—
> Read from the back-page of a paper, say,
>   Held by a neighbor in a subway train,

How at the corner of this avenue
    And such a street (so are the papers filled)
A hurrying man—who happened to be you—
    At noon today had happened to be killed,
I should not cry aloud—I could not cry
    Aloud, or wring my hands in such a place—
I should but watch the station lights rush by
    With a more careful interest on my face,
Or raise my eyes and read with greater care
Where to store furs and how to treat the hair.

The sonnet form is not the only traditional verse form
which Miss Millay uses in her first volume. As a matter
of fact, there is no indication here of that experimentation
in prosody at which other poets were trying their hands;
there are even examples of conventionalized diction and
phrasing which the "new poetry" was bitterly criticizing.
In spite of this, Miss Millay is a new voice. She accepts
no second-hand subject for her poems. She looks within
herself and writes of her own thoughts and feelings. And
she does this with such simplicity and restraint, with so
exact a technique, that she brings a note of freshness, of
youth, of modernity. Consider, for example, "Tavern,"
or "When the Year Grows Old," or the very delicate
"The Little Ghost":

And where the wall is built in new
    And is of ivy bare
She paused—then opened and passed through
    A gate that once was there.

There is in this first book another element which is important because it suggests a trend which some of Miss Millay's later verse was to follow. That is an engaging frankness—at times approaching flippancy—concerning emotions which most people, and particularly most lyric poets, treat only with the greatest seriousness. "Indifference" will serve to illustrate this characteristic. The poet declares an indifference to love that is slow in coming; she will not, as others do, run out to meet him and, when he finally arrives, welcome him with joyous tears. But—as a matter of fact, she lies awake waiting longingly for him; and when he finally does appear, she is more than ready for him, her eyes wet with "the tears some folk might weep!"

This debonair attitude is the forerunner of her second book, which was to express the "Greenwich Village period" of Miss Millay's life and to make her an accepted spokesman for the "new generation." After college, Miss Millay moved to New York and made her home in Greenwich Village "where rents were—in those days—low; in a very tiny room on Waverly Place, hardly large enough for a bed and a typewriter and some cups and saucers; a room, however, with the luxury of a fireplace, for which Joe the Italian brought, every few days, staggering up the stairs, a load of firewood at ten cents a precious stick." [1]

The village, that mad tangle of little streets in lower New York, was just beginning to attract young men and women ambitious to express something new in the arts or in social sciences. To the outsider, it was supposed to be

[1] "The Literary Spotlight," *The Bookman*, November 1922.

a place not wholly respectable, a wild place where adventure lurked. To the dweller within its boundaries, it meant a place of freedom to experiment, a place where new theories might be tried and formulated in sympathetic surroundings. Futuristic pictures were being painted; little theaters were being founded; and the "new poetry" was being written.

So Edna St. Vincent Millay went to Greenwich Village, determined to earn her living by the writing of verse. But though an interest in poetry had begun to revive some few years previous, editors were not any too hospitable to poems or any too generous in paying for accepted ones. Miss Millay's verse was too frequently rejected; her acceptances were too few to assure her an adequate income.

Then her thoughts turned to the theater. Her college dramatic experience must have some value. She applied for positions to various theatrical agents. Finally, she became associated with the Provincetown Players. This group of actors in the summers at Provincetown, Massachusetts, had produced in a new and experimental manner plays written by new and still unrecognized dramatists. Now in Greenwich Village they took an abandoned stable and with a small stage and long, uncomfortable benches converted it into a theater, where their activities might continue throughout the rest of the year. Here Miss Millay acted, and here also some of her own plays were produced.

It was not an easy or a comfortable life that she was leading. There was a false glamor to "Village" life that did not always succeed in transforming poverty, and disappointments, and sorrow. But Miss Millay still found beauty in the world, wrote her poems, and in 1920 gathered them into a volume called *A Few Figs from Thistles*. It is in this book that she is definitely accepted as speaking for the men and women of her generation during those years that immediately followed the great war. The war had shown the inefficacy of old standards of conduct, of old methods of thinking. This encouraged in the new generation the adventuring spirit, the search for new methods, experimentation. But the war had done something more. With appalling suddenness it had cut off the lives of young men—and of young women—before they had had the opportunity to carry out their plans and their dreams. The result, for those that were left, took two forms: they felt a disillusionment and a despair which they sometimes sought to conceal beneath a brave air of flippancy; and they determined to crowd into a certain present what an uncertain future might deny. "Live this life boldly," they said; "but don't be too serious about it."

The opening poems of *A Few Figs*, "First Fig" and "Second Fig," express the attitude succinctly, the celebration of beauty at the expense of foresight and stability. It is expressed again and again, in "Thursday," in "The Penitent," in "She is Overheard Singing," and in Number IV of the group of sonnets, "I shall forget you presently, my dear."

This is a new, or rather a newly expressed, attitude toward love. There is revealed that frankness which was noted in the earlier volume and which admits that, though love itself may be constant, the objects of that love may vary.

This pert and sometimes cynical aspect of Miss Millay's book has called forth fire from many critics. But none can deny the charm and delicacy of some of the poems in this volume. There is a definiteness of characterization in "Portrait by a Neighbor," the picture of a "woman in a dream." And there is an impish wildness in "The Singing-Woman from the Wood's Edge," a poem that possibly explains the conflicting elements in Miss Millay's own verse:

What should I be but a prophet and a liar,
> Whose mother was a leprechaun, whose father was a friar?

It is rather the prophet than the liar who speaks in *Aria da Capo*. This play, published first in *Reedy's Mirror* in St. Louis, printed in London in 1920 in Harold Monro's *The Chapbook*, translated into French and played in Paris, was produced by the Provincetown Players in New York, where Miss Millay's sister, Norma, created the part of Columbine. The play poses against a background of war the frivolous characters of Columbine and Pierrot and the tragic figures of Thyrsis and Corydon.

Columbine and Pierrot open the play with their light, jesting farce. They poke fun at modern poets, musicians, actors, humanitarians, who love humanity but hate people, and critics, for whom enjoyment no longer exists. Their scene is interrupted by Thyrsis and Corydon, who know that it is not yet time for them to appear but who are forced by Cothurnus, the Masque of Tragedy, to play their parts. Out of the game they play grow quarrels. They protest against playing these quarrels seriously; it's only a game, they contend. But Cothurnus, the "inexorable prompter," urges them on. The quarrels turn to bitterness; the two men kill each other.

Pierrot and Columbine return to the stage to resume their act. They object to the disorder caused by the previous scene; the audience, they say, won't countenance their continuing while two dead bodies lie under the table. Cothurnus, from off stage, urges them simply to pull down the tablecloth and thus hide the bodies. The audience, not seeing, he is sure will forget.

This is perhaps somewhat self-conscious art. The play's structure is a little too involved and so not always clear. But the episode of Thyrsis and Corydon is a piece of highly compressed and effective writing; and suggests the origin and growth of wars that nations, themselves, do not want. War, Miss Millay would say, is a folly, a play, a piece for the theater, just as much as is the farcical chatter of Pierrot and of his love.

Another play was written shortly after this period. Miss Millay had left this country for Europe. In Paris, she wrote "The Lamp and the Bell" for the fiftieth anniversary of the founding of the Vassar College Alumnae Association and dedicated it to the class of 1917. The play was produced outdoors at Vassar in June 1921. There are in it some lyrics that are reprinted in a later volume of poetry, *The Harp Weaver*. There are examples of poetic humor:

The woman stirs me to that point
I feel like a carrot in a stew—I boil so
I bump the kettle on all sides.

There are suggestions of that previously expressed attitude toward love; the ending of love, she says, "is no less honest than the coming of it." There is, moreover, a new note, a sense of social consciousness, which Beatrice ruling in Fiori enunciates when she declares that she would prefer that a scoundrel be at liberty rather "than that a just man be punished."

The same year that saw the production of the Vassar play saw the publication of *Second April,* in which the poet reached fuller power and through which she achieved her first real and widespread fame. Here is the poet of *Renascence* grown older and more certain; here are the moods of the first book but with an undertone of dignity. The early ecstasy of "Renascence" is caught in "The Blue-Flag in the Bog"; there is the sense of the brevity of beauty as in "Mariposa." There is the same preoccupation with death; but the passing of beauty and of love has about it now no suspicion of levity. Death can be given a universality as in "Lament"; or it can become a very close, a very personal thing as in "The Poet and His Book" and in the very tender poems making up the *Memorial to D. C.,* to Dorothy Coleman, Vassar 1918, who died a short time after her graduation from college. Whatever the mood may be, there is throughout the book the evidence of fine craftsmanship, an economy of words, a sense of restraint and proportion in expression.

Miss Millay's place in American poetry was now assured. As if to confirm it, came the announcement in May 1923 that the 1922 Pulitzer Prize for poetry was awarded to her poem "The Harp Weaver," a simply told story of mother love that transcends death.

This poem is the title poem for the volume of verse that appeared in 1923. In addition to a number of lyrics, which strike somehow a note of bitterness and disillusionment, there are three noteworthy sections. Part Three shows the poet experimenting with verse forms. Part Five, "Sonnets from An Ungrafted Tree," uses the sonnet —though taking liberty with the length of the last line —to present the clearly defined characters of a woman and her husband and to tell the story of their relationship to each other. It is, however, in the fourth section, in the collection of twenty-two unnamed sonnets, that Miss Millay shows complete mastery of her material. The final sonnet of this group is not without significance, for it shows the poet still worshiping Beauty—a beauty now, however, not of little things but of abstract order and unity: "Euclid alone has looked on Beauty bare."

In 1923 Miss Millay married Eugen Jan Boisseva.n. In June 1925 she received the degree of Litt.D. from Tufts College. And in 1926 there came a story from England that Thomas Hardy, the dean of English letters, had declared that in the United States there were only two great things: what he called our "recessional buildings," and the poetry of Edna St. Vincent Millay.

It is not surprising, then, that when Deems Taylor was commissioned by the Metropolitan Opera Company

to compose an American opera he should have chosen
Miss Millay to write his libretto. Miss Millay worked on
it in her Greenwich Village home, and in the Maine woods.
Finally, in August 1926, she announced its completion.
From the time of this announcement until the premier of
The King's Henchman, on February 17, 1927, the world
of music and of literature waited expectantly, and read
eagerly the advance publicity that flooded the newspapers.
The opening performance, receiving newspaper first-page
prominence, was a gala occasion. The opera, hailed as the
outstanding American opera, was most enthusiastically
received.

But what of the play? *The King's Henchman* is a tale
of tenth-century England, a variation of the Tristram
motif. King Eadgar sends his foster-brother Aethelwold,
a warrior uninterested in women, to woo on his behalf
Aelfrida, the daughter of Ordgar, Thane of Devon. In
the mists of the forest on All Hallow Eve, Aethelwold
and his servant Maccus lose their way. While Maccus sets
off to see if he can find the road, Aethelwold falls asleep
and is discovered by Aelfrida, who "in spell and rune"
has been seeking a lover. Aethelwold awakes and, overwhelmed by the woman's beauty, falls in love with her.
He learns her identity; but, forgetful of his loyalty to
his king, determines to wed her and to send Maccus back
to Eadgar with the message that Aelfrida is not the sort
of woman to make a royal bride. When the last act opens,
Aethelwold and Aelfrida have been married for some
time, but have not found happiness. Aethelwold is restless
and filled with remorse; Aelfrida is discontented that she

must remain in her father's home. They finally decide to leave England. But before they can put their plan into effect, word comes that Eadgar is on his way to visit his foster-brother. Filled with dismay, Aethelwold confesses to Aelfrida the tale of his treachery and the fact that but for the mist which had first brought them together she might have been queen of England; he begs her to make herself unattractive when the king arrives so that his secret may be kept. But Aelfrida, persuaded half by her servant Ase, half by her own ambition and discontent, appears before the king radiantly dressed, more beautiful than ever! Eadgar is at first bewildered and then realizes what had occurred. And Aethelwold, eager to atone in the only way that now seems open to him, draws his dagger and kills himself.

As a play, *The King's Henchman* has but few dramatic moments. As an opera, its poetic virtue, the skillful use of Saxon speech, presents a damaging drawback. Can one imagine the difficulty of singing "Sawst thou ever the moss so sea-weed sodden wet?" or "Now hath his Lady a bitter burthen to thole!"?

But, as poetry, it contains those apt humorous figures that have been noted before. Maccus, the "bearded nightingale," declares, "My heart hath a stone in its shoes." And it contains, particularly in the forest love scene, many passages of great lyric beauty. It would seem, indeed, that Miss Millay's gift is not a great dramatic gift; but rather a personal one, one of self-revelation.

During the years of poetic creation, Miss Millay's life was not limited by the covers of her books. The world

outside was claiming her attention. In the public senti-
ment aroused by the Sacco-Vanzetti trial and conviction,
she found an opportunity to express her interest in public
affairs. The two men had been accused and convicted of
murder; they had been sentenced to death. But there were
elements in the trial itself, peculiarities of Massachusetts
legal technicalities, that suggested that there might have
been a miscarriage of justice. Liberal-minded people of
the United States banded themselves together for the
defense of the two men. Among these was Miss Millay.
In August 1927, on the eve of the men's execution, demon-
strations of protest were held. Miss Millay took an active
part in one of the parades, carrying a banner with the
words, "If these men are executed, Justice is dead in
Massachusetts." She was arrested for disturbing the peace
and fined.

Her indignation was not a temporary one. To *The Outlook* for November 9, 1927, she contributed an article
entitled "Fear." In it she made a significant statement.
"The world," she says, "the physical world, and that
once was all in all to me, has at moments such as these no
roads through a wood, no stretch of shore, that can bring
me comfort. The beauty of these things can no longer at
such moments make up to me at all for the ugliness of
man, his cruelty, his greed, his lying face." To Miss
Millay now, something is more important than mere physical beauty!

Her poem, "Justice Denied in Massachusetts," written
as her "contribution to the registering of the feeling many
of us have about the Sacco-Vanzetti execution," appears

in her latest volume, *The Buck in the Snow*. This book, published in 1928, was written for the most part in her studio on her farm at Austerlitz, New York, near Massachusetts. The studio adjoins an old barn across the road from the poet's farmhouse and is built in the treetops, its floors resting on the branches.

The book seems a recapitulation of all the earlier moods and thoughts of the poet. There is still the longing for the sea, as in "Mist in the Valley." There is still the insistence of life as in "Moriturus," a defiance and protest against death that is repeated in "Dirge Without Music"—

I am not resigned to the shutting away of loving hearts
    in the hard ground.—

an exultation in the temporary victory Love may claim over death, as in "Sonnet"—

Death is our master,—but his seat is shaken;
He rides victorious,—but his ranks are thinned.

There is the same succinct beauty of expression, as in the title poem of the book. There is the same mastery of the sonnet and the same worship of an ideal, these two combined in the superb "Sonnet to Gath." But even this poem suggests a deeper note, a note of disenchantment and despair, but one that is tempered with pity and sympathy. Her despair reaches its depth in "The Anguish":

The anguish of the world is on my tongue.
My bowl is filled to the brim with it; there is more than
    I can eat.

EDNA ST. VINCENT MILLAY

Miss Millay has grown older. But she is still young. And one feels that the key of her singing has not been irrevocably set. Perhaps it never will be. For she is a creature of moods and of quickly changing emotions. And she will sing her own songs in her own way. But of one thing one can be almost sure; there will be a glorious confidence expressed in her songs, a challenge to a full and rich life, a ringing call to

Take up the song; forget the epitaph.

POETICAL WORKS

RENASCENCE	*Harper and Brothers*
A FEW FIGS FROM THISTLES	*Harper and Brothers*
SECOND APRIL	*Harper and Brothers*
THREE PLAYS	*Harper and Brothers*
THE HARP WEAVER	*Harper and Brothers*
THE KING'S HENCHMAN	*Harper and Brothers*
THE BUCK IN THE SNOW	*Harper and Brothers*
EDNA ST. VINCENT MILLAY'S POEMS SELECTED FOR YOUNG PEOPLE	*Harper and Brothers*

EDWIN ARLINGTON ROBINSON

EDWIN ARLINGTON ROBINSON

O NE of Edwin Arlington Robinson's earliest memories is that of sitting on the floor and reciting to his mother Thomas Campbell's sonorous poem, "Lochiel's Warning." Picture a little boy repeating the tale of a wizard who warns a Scottish chieftain against going forth to battle, prophesying for him cruel defeat and a crueller death. Imagine a young voice mouthing the stilted language of the warning:

> Life flutters convulsed in his quivering limbs,
> And his blood-streaming nostril in agony swims,
> Accursed be the faggots, that blaze at his feet,
> Where his heart shall be thrown, ere it ceases to beat.
> With the smoke of its ashes to poison the gale . . .

Need one be told that Lochiel, undaunted, declares, "Down, soothless insulter! I trust not the tale!" and announces his decision to fight, regardless of the outcome?

> While the kindling of life in his bosom remains
> Shall victor exult, or in death be laid low
> With his back to the field, and his feet to the foe!
> And leaving in battle no blot on his name,
> Look proudly to Heaven from the death-bed of fame.

Had some wizard been present when this poem was being declaimed, he might have been able to foretell something of the little boy's future. So early an introduction to poetry must develop into a lifelong interest; any wizard could tell that. A very skillful one might have seen more and might have recognized in Lochiel's defiant determination a pattern of conduct and thought which the young Robinson was to follow. For as a young man, Robinson wholeheartedly dedicated himself to poetry; he could not be swerved from his purpose by the criticism—or by the indifference—of the public; and he refused to be influenced by what he considered the accidents of time and of place, by local customs, or by changing habits of thought. With Robinson, life and poetry merged into one entity; and since it was his poems that expressed the fundamental truths of his life, these to him seemed more important than the dates at which he happened to do certain things, or than the things themselves!

Such steady devotion led, not unnaturally, to marked achievement in his work. And such indifference to the details of individual existence led just as surely to silence on the part of the poet concerning his personal life. As a result, it has been said of Robinson, "He is not only the best, he is the most reticent, poet." In fact the word *reticent,* or some synonym for it, is the one most frequently encountered when Robinson is the subject of discussion.

An anonymous writer in *The Bookman* for January 1923 succeeds in painting a word-picture of the man that any one might see:

"He has his own circle of friends and he is a welcome

adjunct to their gatherings, although he much prefers to sit and listen rather than talk.

"A tall, slender man. A high forehead with dark thinning hair. Quiet contemplative eyes which peer through spectacles. A short dark mustache (English fashion) barely concealing a thin secretive mouth. A gravity of demeanor that often breaks into a smile which trembles curiously about the mouth. He dresses quietly, generally in dark clothes, and always carries a cane. When he walks, he stoops slightly, the droop of a scholar who is an inveterate reader. He hates to walk. He wears a soft hat."

But the same writer, in seeking from the poet an explanation of the inner man, could get only vague hints and shy indications:

"He once stated that he descended from good New England stock. This is suggestion number one. His boyhood was a rather lonely one. This is suggestion number two. He loves to be exact in his reasoning and to settle questions to his own satisfaction. Suggestion number three. He once said that if he were placed on a desert island and permitted but three books for the remainder of his life, he should choose the Bible, Shakespeare, and the dictionary. There is suggestion number four. He has never married and has no intention of marrying. Suggestion number five. His favorite writer of fiction is Charles Dickens. He professes a profound admiration for the poetry of William Wordsworth. He takes off his soft hat to Thomas Hardy. In New York, he rises late and generally goes to bed long after midnight. He adores detective stories and Sherlock Holmes is one of his heroes. He is absolutely immune to cults, isms, and movements. Surely these scattered facts are streams pointing to the personality of the man."

Fortunately, there is some further information with which these uncoördinated facts can be supplemented; and if a complete picture can not be painted, yet there can be sketched the outline of the man's external life.

That life began on December 22, 1869, in the little Maine town of Head Tide, where Edward Robinson, the poet's father, was a grain merchant. A year or two after his son's birth, the father was made a director of the bank at Gardiner, Maine, whither he moved with his family.

Gardiner is situated on the north bank of the Kennebec River, and is the "Tilbury Town" of Robinson's poetry. Here Robinson felt that atmosphere which was to dominate his poems—a sense of an old order trying to maintain itself against the onrush of time. The town, like a bit of transplanted England, possessed its manor house, the home of the Gardiner family; but at the time of the poet's boyhood, the Gardiner fortune was not flourishing and the house stood an empty symbol of past grandeur, unable to fulfill its function in the present.

At Gardiner, too, Robinson saw and came to know truly those men and women in whom he found the material for his poetry and his philosophy. Here must have lived men like Aaron Stark—

> A miser was he, with a miser's nose,
> And eyes like little dollars in the dark;

and Uncle Ananias—

> Out of all ancient men my childhood knew
> I choose him and I mark him for the best.
> Of all authoritative liars, too,
> I crown him loveliest;

and women like Pamela of "The Tree in Pamela's
Garden"—

> Her neighbors—doing all that neighbors can
> To make romance of reticence meanwhile—
> Seeing that she had never loved a man,
> Wished Pamela had a cat, or a small bird,
> And only would have wondered at her smile
> Could they have seen that she had overheard.

Here, as a matter of fact, he did know Laura E. Richards,
the daughter of Julia Ward Howe, and herself a writer
of children's books. "Aunt Laura" had a club, of which
the sole purpose was the telling of stories, and of which
Edwin Arlington was a loyal member.

It was the local Gardiner schools that Robinson attended
until, in 1891, he entered Harvard. But his college training was brief. After two years he was called back to
Gardiner by his father's illness, and from that time formal education ceased.

During his boyhood and early manhood, his interest
in verse had become crystallized and he had written a
number of poems. Some, incidentally, were written in the
barn of his Gardiner home. A critical attitude toward his
own work made him destroy much of his writing. But of

what was left there was enough material for a small privately printed volume, a slim blue book, called *The Torrent and the Night Before*, and dedicated "to any man, woman or critic who will cut the edges of it. I have done the top." Although only five hundred and fifty copies were printed, three years did not exhaust the edition. Now the book is a valuable collector's item. Even so well-known a bibliophile as Amy Lowell was unable to secure a copy.

One copy, however, must have fallen into the hands of a critic who did deign to cut the pages. For the February 1897 issue of *The Bookman* reviewed it:

"There is true fire in his verse and there are the swing and the singing of wind and wave and the passion of human emotion in his lines; but his limitations are vital. His humor is of a grim sort and the world is not beautiful to him, but a prison-house. In the night-time there is weeping and sorrow, and joy does not come in the morning. But here and there in a sonnet he lets himself go, and the cry of a yearning spirit enters the lute of Orpheus and sounds a sweet and wondrous note."

In the following number of the magazine, under "Chronicle and Comment," the editor notes that Robinson both expressed his thanks for the "unexpected notice" of his book and at the same time denied the charge of pessimism: "I am sorry to learn that I have painted myself in such lugubrious colours. The world is not a 'prison-house' but a kind of spiritual kindergarten, where millions of bewildered infants are trying to spell God with the wrong blocks."

There is deep significance in this reply of the poet. For this note of bewilderment, of a handicapped search for an ideal, is a keynote for all his poetry.

Besides *The Bookman's* critic, a few others read the book, and also read *The Children of the Night,* which appeared in 1897 and which included some of the earlier poems. Among these readers were J. S. Barstow and H. H. Richards, the son of "Aunt Laura," both residents of Gardiner and both students at Harvard a few years after Robinson had left the university. These men delightedly quoted lines from Robinson's poems to a third classmate, Fullerton Waldo. It is to him that we owe a description of Robinson during his visits to Harvard in 1897-98 and during the ten obscure years that followed.[1]

"One day there came a tapping at my chamber door —41 Thayer—and Robinson's hesitant head and penetrant dark eyes behind their glasses poked in. In his hand he had one of those 'words and music' librettos which they sell in the lobby at the opera. It was Balfe's 'Bohemian Girl.' 'Will you play these to me?' he asked with a fascinating smile that came and went with a spot of color in each cheek.

"There were three things he wanted: 'I dreamt I dwelt in marble halls,' 'The heart bowed down,' 'When other lips and other hands.' These I played over and over. He never grew tired of them. Often after that he came and I tried to play them as if they were forever fresh and new."

[1] "The Earlier Edwin Arlington Robinson—Some Memories of a Poet in the Making," *The Outlook,* November 30, 1921.

Shortly after, Robinson left New England to go to New York, which was gradually taking its place as the literary center of America. So 1900 found Robinson close to New York City, in Yonkers, where, a few years before, another poet, John Masefield, had been at work in a carpet factory. Robinson's home was a small room in a house opposite a factory, on a mean, cobbled street. At Yonkers his friends numbered Mr. Waldo, William Vaughn Moody, the poet, and Daniel Gregory Mason, the musician. With them, for the sake of his health, he took long walks, during which he formulated his views on life in general and on poetry in particular.

He held a firm belief that poetry could be made his means of livelihood. Made hopeful by the example of another poet and yet awestruck by that poet's fortune, he once said, "Clinton Scollard, I am told, earns $1200 a year." He expressed his indifference to public recognition. But this was not made an excuse for indifference to the demands of his art; he insisted always on conscientious effort and perfect craftsmanship.

The poems on which he was then working appeared in 1902 in his *Captain Craig*. Still, public interest was not aroused.

About this time Robinson moved to West Twenty-third Street, New York City, to a room with a bed, a chair, a mirrorless bureau, and a washstand with a cracked water-pitcher. Here in the hurry and confusion of a restless metropolis, Robinson found and maintained the calm and seclusion that have always been so necessary to him. Here, too, by a similar contradictory twist of fate, he, the meditative, intellectual poet, found work checking off loads of stone for the New York subway, then being built.

But soon there came a change of fortune. In 1905 a second edition of *The Children of the Night* was published, which in due time came to the attention of President Roosevelt, who was an insatiable reader, and delighted particularly in the discovery of previously unknown authors. The book pleased him; and he took time to review it for *The Outlook* of August 12.

"There is an undoubted touch of genius in the poems collected in this volume and a curious simplicity and good faith, all of which qualities differentiate them sharply from ordinary collections of the kind. There is in them just a little of the light that never was on land or sea and in such light the objects described often have nebulous outlines; but it is not always necessary in order to enjoy a poem that one should be able to translate it into terms of mathematical accuracy."

The review ends on a questioning note that has since been satisfactorily answered: "Mr. Robinson has written in this little volume not verse but poetry. Whether he has the power of sustained flight remains to be seen."

With characteristic energy, the President set about finding a position in which he might place Robinson where, secure from the fear of want, he could continue to write his poetry. One day when Richard Watson Gilder, the editor, was having lunch at the White House, the President suddenly demanded, "What shall we do with Robinson?" He could not conceive of the possibility that any one should not know which Robinson was meant. After various suggestions had been discussed and abandoned, it was decided to offer him a consulship in Mexico.

But one element necessary to the plan's success had not been considered, and that element was the poet himself. Robinson refused to leave New York! The President, not to be deterred from his purpose, finally secured for him a position in the New York Customs House. It is a question how valuable Robinson's services were to the government. Robinson, himself, declared that he was "the least efficient public servant who ever drew his pay from the United States Treasury Department." There is a story that so desultory was his interest in his work that his superior once wrote him a note suggesting that he appear at his desk at least frequently enough to receive his salary!

In 1909 even such casual labor grew distasteful, and Robinson resigned from his position to give all his time and energy to the creation of poetry. From this point on, the important facts in Robinson's life are his poems; the significant dates, those when his books were published. Robinson, definitely abandoning all careers but that of poetry, must now be considered as Robinson the poet.

What is his relationship to other poets?

When Robinson first began to write, poetry in America had fallen into a decline. People were writing pale imitations of earlier poets, elaborating fancies and conceits, intrigued more with manner than with subject. Into this heavy, stifled air, Robinson came as a fresh breeze. His poetry was definitely his own, individual, original, and *modern*.

These characteristics manifest themselves in the 1905

edition of *The Children of the Night,* which contains some poems that have not been surpassed in any later volume, and which shows markedly the definite trend that all his work was to follow. In the first place, it is evident that Robinson feels that the subject matter for poetry is not limited; the experiences of everyday life are its fit material. So his poems, for the most part, owe their origin to the men and women whom he knew in youth and to the philosophical questionings that perplexed him. In manner, too, there is a break from earlier writers. While he does not reject the gains to be got from an allusive quality in verse, he uses little "poetic diction" and he permits no distortion of accent or word order for the sake of rhythm. His rhythm is the rhythm of speech.

At the same time Robinson must not be considered a leader of the "new poetry." Whatever his influence has been—and he began writing and publishing a good fifteen years before the beginning of that movement—he has never had any conscious connection with any group. Unlike the "new poets," he has not felt himself hampered by old verse forms; rather, he molds them to his own use. So he uses the quatrain and ballad stanza, the ballade, and the villanelle. A lilting form like the triolet becomes the vehicle for a mood of desolation, as in "The House on the Hill." The restricting sonnet is used to analyze character, to lay bare and explain the soul of man.

REUBEN BRIGHT

Because he was a butcher and thereby
Did earn an honest living (and did right),
I would not have you think that Reuben Bright
Was any more a brute than you or I;
For when they told him that his wife must die,
He stared at them, and shook with grief and fright,
And cried like a great baby half that night,
And made the women cry to see him cry.

And after she was dead, and he had paid
The singers and the sexton and the rest,
He packed a lot of things that she had made
Most mournfully away in an old chest
Of hers, and put some chopped-up cedar boughs
In with them, and tore down to the slaughter-house.

Nor is he, as the "new poets" are, a rebel. He is not
concerned with the effects that the temporary modes of
civilization have upon man. He looks beneath the world
of change for the lasting and permanent influences and
finds them in man's own character. And so he uses little
local color. He removes his men and women from a definite setting. They are not New Englanders, they are Man
Universal. Richard Cory, for example, might have lived
in any time and in any place.

EDWIN ARLINGTON ROBINSON

RICHARD CORY

Whenever Richard Cory went down town,
We people on the pavement looked at him:
He was a gentleman from sole to crown,
Clean-favored, and imperially slim.

And he was always quietly arrayed,
And he was always human when he talked;
But still he fluttered pulses when he said,
"Good-morning," and he glittered when he walked.

And he was rich—yes, richer than a king—
And admirably schooled in every grace:
In fine, we thought that he was every thing
To make us wish that we were in his place.

So on we worked, and waited for the light,
And went without the meat, and cursed the bread;
And Richard Cory, one calm summer night,
Went home and put a bullet through his head.

It is in these pen-pictures that Robinson excels. There are few details. All non-essentials are stripped away. The reader must supplement from his sympathies and imagination what the poet writes. Yet with intense dramatic effect he succeeds in making a single act reveal a whole life!

Richard Cory suggests the type of man with whom Robinson is most concerned. He is one of life's failures, and it is they whom one meets again and again throughout the poet's books. For Robinson such men fall into two classes. One is made up of those who, like Cory, are judged successes by the world but who are nevertheless spiritual failures. The others are those who

> Beloved of none, forgot by many,
> Dismissed as an inferior wraith
> Reborn may be as great as any.

Paralleling this concern with man, there is Robinson's concern with the problem of the universe. His poem "Credo," which appears in this volume, is important because it shows his fundamental philosophy:

> I cannot find my way: there is no star
> In all the shrouded heavens anywhere;
> And there is not a whisper in the air
> Of any living voice but one so far
> That I can hear it only as a bar
> Of lost, imperial music, played when fair
> And angel fingers wove, and unaware,
> Dead leaves to garlands where no roses are.
>
> No, there is not a glimmer, nor a call,
> For one that welcomes, welcomes when he fears,
> The black and awful chaos of the night;
> For through it all—above, beyond it all—
> I know the far-sent message of the years,
> I feel the coming glory of the Light.

The title poem of *Captain Craig*, which had appeared in 1902, is a long, at times wearisome, poem of an outcast

supported by four young men. But though Captain Craig
is a worldly failure, he is saved from spiritual defeat:

> I cannot think of anything to-day
> That I would rather do than be myself.

He suggests the active element of Robinson's philosophy
in his admonition:

> So climb high,
> And having set your steps regard not much
> The downward laughter clinging at your feet,
> Nor overmuch the warning; only know,
> As well as you know dawn from lantern-light,
> That far above you, for you, and within you,
> There burns and shines and lives, unwavering
> And always yours, the truth.

In 1910, there appeared *The Town Down the River*,
the poet's name for New York. The book was dedicated
to President Roosevelt and contained a poem about him,
"The Revealer." There were, in addition, two other
studies of public men: one of Napoleon in "An Island,"
and the other, most successful, of Lincoln in "The
Master."

The following year, Robinson made a discovery that
was to mean much to him. He found the MacDowell
Colony at Peterborough, New Hampshire. There Mrs.
Edward MacDowell, the widow of the composer, had
established a settlement where American artists, compos-

ers, and writers might work under ideal conditions. This is the manner of the discovery as Robinson tells it.[2]

. . . "I found myself in possession of a thing I was pleased to call an idea for a Work of Art, and one that required, for its most advantageous working out, a combination of conditions that was not promised by the sights, smells, temperatures, and noises of New York City during the Summer months, or by any enforced seclusion that I had then in mind.

"What I required, or at least wished for, was a place in the country, not too far from the civilizing conveniences of life, that would afford comfortable lodging, good food, a large and well-windowed sleeping room with a good bed in it, an easy walk to breakfast at about seven-thirty, a longer walk to a secluded and substantial building in the woods, a large open fireplace and plenty of fuel, a free view from the door of the best kind of New England scenery, a complete assurance of a long day before me without social annoyance or interruptions of any kind, a simple luncheon brought to my door by a punctual but reticent carrier, a good dinner at night with a few congenial people, an evening without enforced solitude or enforced society, and blessed assurance that no one would ask me to show him or her what I was writing."

All these requirements were met by Peterborough, where Robinson found the opportunity "to get away for awhile from the world and to express a part of what the world had given me." At Peterborough he became "Merlin playing pool." There he was happy. And so since

2 "The Peterborough Idea," *North American Review*, September 1916.

1911 there he has spent his summers, living during the winter in New York.

After writing two prose plays, *Van Zorn* and *The Porcupine*, Robinson produced a volume of poems that was to mark the turning-point in critical praise. *The Man Against the Sky*, 1916, received the wholehearted approval of the critics. "In reading it," Amy Lowell wrote, "one experiences a sensation akin to that of the man who opens a jar of compressed air. It is a profound wonder that so much can have been forced into so small a space."

Again in this volume are word-portraits: "The man Flammonde, from God knows where," who exerted a powerful influence on those with whom he came in contact; Old King Cole who, unperturbed, listened to those who complained of the misdeeds of his "two disastrous heirs," and to critics or sympathizers said:

> And if I'd rather live than weep
> Meanwhile, do you find that surprising?
> Why, bless my soul, the man's asleep!
> That's good, the sun will soon be rising.

There is Bewick Finzer, who, having wasted his fortune, comes begging a loan:

> Familiar as an old mistake,
> And futile as regret.

The most successful portrait is that in "Ben Jonson Entertains a Man from Stratford." It is a picture of Shakespeare as Jonson sees him:

Tell me, now,
If ever there was anything let loose
On earth by gods or devils heretofore
Like this mad, careful, proud, indifferent Shakespeare.

In this poem Robinson performs the difficult feat of putting the thoughts that are troubling him into words that Shakespeare might have used:

It's Nothing. It's all Nothing.
We come, we go; and when we're done, we're done;
Spiders and flies—we're mostly one or t'other—
We come, we go; and when we're done, we're done.

It is in the title poem of this volume that one finds Robinson's own answer to his perplexity. A symbol of all mankind is the man who stood revealed against the sky

As if he were the last god going home
Unto his last desire.

Dark, marvelous, and inscrutable he moved on
Till down the fiery distance he was gone.

Robinson's—and mankind's—final answer is this:

Where was he going, this man against the sky?
You know not, nor do I.
But this we know, if we know anything:
That we may laugh and fight and sing
And of our transcience here make offering
To an orient Word that will not be erased,

> Or, save in incommunicable gleams
> Too permanent for dreams,
> Be found or known.

In spite of questions that cannot be answered, Robinson maintains that something within man himself prevents complete pessimism and loss of hope. The mere persistence of life proves that all does not "come to Nought"; faith must be stronger than reason.

With *Merlin*, in 1917, came the first of the retellings of the Arthurian legends. Robinson seeks not to give the richly embroidered pageantry of the legendary age, but to recast the old story in terms of the present. It is the tale of the decay of Arthur's kingdom. It is Merlin's tragedy that he

> saw too far
> But not so far as this.

He foresees the changes in the kingdom; but he is unable to help Arthur, who has retained his boyhood faith in the wizard. He sees, too, that time will change his relationship with Vivian; but he decides:

> I see no more for me to do
> Than to leave her and Arthur and the world
> Behind me, and to pray that all be well
> With Vivian.

The force of the theme is weakened, however, by defects in the poem's structure: a lagging plot, delay of action, and hazy time-sequence.

In spite of this, the book was well noticed. It was becoming now a literary habit for each new volume of Robinson to receive—and to receive deservedly—an increased measure of praise.

The poet's fiftieth birthday evoked such praise of the man and of his work as has seldom, if ever, been duplicated. Writers, conservative like Edwin Markham, or radical, like Vachel Lindsay and Amy Lowell, joined in honoring him. Newspapers and magazines printed laudatory editorials and articles, which must have brought immeasurable pleasure to the man "who is understood to be rather careless of approbation or of blame."

In the following year two volumes appeared: *The Three Taverns* and, continuing the Arthurian tradition, *Lancelot*. *The Three Taverns* again contains studies of historical characters: Paul in the title poem, Hamilton and Burr in "On the Way," and John Brown in a poem of that name. The last-named poem repeats Robinson's conviction of individuality:

> Meanwhile, I've a strange content,
> A patience, and a vast indifference
> To what men say of me and what men fear
> To say.

It ends with the ringing line: "I shall have more to say when I am dead." "The Mill," in this volume, is an excellent example of Robinson's ability to compress intensely a whole story into a short poem, and furnishes a striking contrast to the handling of plot in *Merlin*.

Lancelot, which won the Lyric Prize, goes on with the

story of Arthur's Court, of the love between Lancelot and Guinevere, of an old order changing and of old ideals disappearing. It is possible that the great war influenced Robinson and moved him to write:

> What are kings?
> And how much longer are there to be kings?
> When are the millions who are now like worms
> To know that kings are worms, if they are worms?

But it is just as probable that had there been no war, the poem would have been the same: for *Lancelot* is primarily another statement of Robinson's fundamental thought:

> There was nothing.
> But always in the darkness he rode on,
> Alone; and in the darkness came the Light.

The title poem of *Avon's Harvest*, 1921, Robinson calls a "dime novel in verse." It is the analysis of a character who carried from childhood to death a schoolboy hatred and fear. In contrast to the tense, overwhelming tragic sense of this poem is the delicate, whimsical treatment of "Mr. Flood's Party," in which lonely Mr. Flood invites himself to a carousal.

> "Well, Mr. Flood, we have not met like this
> In a long time; and many a change has come
> To both of us, I fear, since last it was
> We had a drop together. Welcome home!"
> Convivially returning with himself,
> Again he raised the jug up to the light;

And with an acquiescent quaver said:
"Well, Mr. Flood, if you insist, I might."

The product of his years of writing Robinson revised
and brought out in the volume of *Collected Poems* in
1921. In the following January, the Authors Club of
New York voted this book the most notable publication
of the preceding year, and to commemorate its award
issued a book on the life and work of the poet. In May
he was awarded the Pulitzer Prize for poetry. And in
June he slipped away from Peterborough, to return
shortly after, embarrassed and reticent as ever, after having received from Yale the honorary degree of LL.D.
Surely one might say that he had achieved fame! But that
Fame had come with laggard feet is shown in an article
by John Drinkwater in the *Fortnightly Review* for April
1921, which speaks of Robinson as "little known in America, in England hardly more than a name."

That name was to become better known. Each succeeding book was to have an increasing number of readers.
Roman Bartholow, 1923, dedicated to Percy Mackaye,
is the story of Roman, of his wife Gabrielle, and his friend
Penn-Raven. Penn-Raven has cured Bartholow of some
strange mental disorder, and then has fallen in love with
Bartholow's wife. Gabrielle, who has not been able to
lead a happy existence with Bartholow, sees no hope for
happiness with Penn-Raven and so commits suicide. Dom-
inating the book, commenting on the incidents, is the quaint
and almost grotesque fisher-philosopher, Umfraville.

In 1924 for a second time the Pulitzer Prize was awarded to Robinson, this time for *The Man Who Died Twice*. Fernando Nash,

> Where former dominance and authority
> Had now disintegrated, lapsed, and shrunken
> To an inferior mystery that had yet
> The presence in defeat . . .

dissipated his life and his musical genius. After a debauch, he has what seems to him a vision of his place in life:

> At last alive, it was enough to serve,
> And so to be content where God should call him.

He joins the band of the Salvation Army, praising the Lord to the beating of his drum, and dies at last—his second death—with no regret:

> And fear not for my soul. I have found that,
> Though I have lost all else!

Another of Robinson's failures who transcend failure!

Dionysus in Doubt, 1925, may have been prompted by the prohibition amendment. It is in any case a protest against laws compelling uniformity of thought and conduct, a reversion to the old theme of individuality. The book contains, in addition to several long poems, a number of sonnets, the medium in which Robinson finds himself so happy. These, together with those from his

earlier books, he was later to gather into a single volume
and publish in 1928 under the simple title of *Sonnets.*

A new height in Robinson's career was reached with
the publication of *Tristram* in 1927. On May 9, the day
before the book was given to the public, a group of Robinson's friends met in the Little Theatre, New York, to
hear Mrs. August Belmont read to them the tale of Tristram, of his love for Isolt of Ireland, the bride of his
Uncle Mark, of his banishment from Cornwall, and of
his marriage to Isolt of Brittany, "Isolt of the white
hands." Tristram, called back to Arthur's kingdom, returns to the dark Isolt. The two lovers are murdered by
Andred, acting from a false sense of loyalty to King
Mark; while Mark, who has realized his inability to win
Isolt's love and has acknowledged the overwhelming
power of her love for Tristram, can only say of them:

"I should say fate was mightier than I was.

I am not sure that you have not done well.
God knows what you have done. I do not know."

So brief an outline of the poem can give but a faint
suggestion of its force. The moving love story is told
without any of the medieval trappings that are wont to
accompany the Tristram legend; its emphasis is placed
on the delineation of character and of emotion. The passionate love of Tristram and the Irish Isolt is contrasted,
now with the jealous treacherous wiles of Queen Morgan,
now with the light cavalier attitude of Gawaine, and
finally, with that confident, tender love of the fair Isolt:

                            He had been all,
And would be always all there was for her,
And he had not come back to her alive,
Not even to go again. It was like that
For women, sometimes, and might be so too often
For women like her. She hoped there were not many
Of them, or many of them to be, not knowing
More about that than about waves and foam,
And white birds everywhere, flying, and flying;
Alone, with her white face and her gray eyes,
She watched them there till even her thoughts were white,
And there was nothing alive but white birds flying,
Flying, and always flying, and still flying,
And the white sunlight flashing on the sea.

The poignant story revealed a new Robinson. The same
sympathy and understanding of character were present;
but the detached and intellectual analysis and presentation
gave way to a depth and warmth of feeling until then
little suspected. Because of this and its indisputable literary excellence, *Tristram* was chosen by the Literary Guild
as one of its books and so Robinson reached—at last—
a public that might not otherwise have known him.

In November Robinson was elected to the American
Academy of Arts and Letters; and in May 1928 he re-
ceived for the third time the Pulitzer award. Surely,
Fame had at last forced itself upon the poet!

Why should general recognition, so remarkable when
it finally arrived, have been so slow in coming? In the

first place, there was Robinson's indifference to the public. This must not be construed into a lack of faith in his poetry. Of that he once said, "It seems to me that poetry has two characteristics. One is that it is, after all, indefinable. The other is that it is eventually unmistakable." If this is true eventually of poetry, the poet, Robinson would say, need not be impatient; he can afford to wait.

Before he received general approbation, he was called the poet for the few, the poet of the mind. He was accused of being abstruse; his poems were criticized as being difficult to understand. To this Robinson replied, one can imagine a little wearily, "Why cannot they read one word after another?"

The obvious rejoinder to this is that frequently the words are not there. In the elimination of details, in the suppression of the obvious, Robinson can be effective, as, for example, in "Two Gardens in Linndale," wherein the death of one brother is told in these stanzas:

> Year after year 'twas all the same:
> With none to envy, none to blame,
> They lived along in innocence,
> Nor ever once forgot the fence,
> Till on a day the Stranger came.

> He came to greet them where they were,
> And he too was a Gardener:
> He stood between these gentle men,
> He stayed a little while, and then
> The land was all for Oliver.

On the other hand, the result can be as baffling as the sonnet, "Not Always":

> In surety and obscurity twice mailed,
> And first achieving with initial rout
> A riddance of weak fear and weaker doubt,
> He strode alone. But when too long assailed
> By nothing, even a stronger might have quailed
> As he did, and so might have gazed about
> Where he could see the last light going out,
> Almost as if the fire of God had failed.
>
> And so it was till out of silence crept
> Invisible avengers of a name
> Unknown, like jungle-hidden jaguars.
> But there were others coming who had kept
> Their watch and word; and out of silence came
> A song somewhat as of the morning stars.

Again the poet comments: "In real poetry you find that something has been said and yet you find also about it a sort of nimbus of what can't be said." What are the elements of beauty that make up that nimbus and that repay a close reader and student of the poetry?

There is, first, the rhythm of his poetry, the music, as in these lines from "John Evereldown":

> Where are you going to-night, to-night—
>   Where are you going, John Evereldown?
> There's never the sign of a star in sight,
>   Nor a lamp that's nearer than Tilbury Town.

Then there are bright flashes of phrases that illuminate thought: "There were pensioners of dreams and there were debtors of illusions," "At someone's tinkling afternoon at home," "Flame-shaken gloom," "The green beginning of another summer." Even the lengthy and sometimes wearisome passages of the longer poems contain unforgettable lines:

> Your low voice tells how bells of singing gold
> Would sound through twilight over silent water.

> And all that clamor of infernal joy
> That once had shrilled above him and Isolt,
> Were somewhere miles away among the ages
> That he had walked and counted with his feet.

Pervading much of the poetry is a sense of brooding mystery, of light shut out by thick trees. It may be the essential element in a short poem like "Stafford's Cabin":

Once there was a cabin here, and once there was a man; And something happened here before my memory began. Time has made the two of them the fuel of one flame And all we have of them is now a legend and a name.

Or it may be the background atmosphere of a long poem like *Merlin*. But never does the mystery take the form of the supernatural; it is always the mystery of changes through the years, of destiny working itself out through time.

It is particularly in the working out of destiny in the lives of men that Robinson manifests his greatest dramatic power. He uses historical types, like Hood, Crabbe, Erasmus, or Lincoln; legendary ones, like Lancelot, Tristram, Arthur; and imaginary ones, like Flammonde or Aaron Stark, who possess as much reality as do the men of history. In fact, one feels that Robinson creates few characters; he analyzes existing ones.

The type that one finds again and again, it may be repeated, is the failure, the frustrated. But there is never bitterness in the delineation; gentleness is always present. The mood may vary from the tenderness of Pamela and of Mr. Flood to the humor of Miniver Cheevy, "child of scorn"—

> Miniver loved the Medici,
>   Albeit he had never seen one;
> He would have sinned incessantly
>   Could he have been one. . . .
>
> Miniver Cheevy, born too late,
>   Scratched his head and kept on thinking;
> Miniver coughed, and called it fate,
>   And kept on drinking.

On these people, Robinson says we cannot pass judgment. We do not know enough.

> We cannot measure what the world has lost
> Until we know the gauge the builders use
> Who made it. All we know about the world
> For certain is that it appears to be.

Again the bewildered child plays with the wrong kindergarten blocks! One is overwhelmed by doubt and

uncertainty concerning the purpose of the universe. But
the resulting philosophy need not, and ought not, be one
of pessimism or of passivity:

> I do not see myself as one who says
> To man that he shall sit with folded hands
> Against the Coming.

The one figure that Robinson continually employs is
that of a gleam, a guiding light. It is the light of truth,
truth to oneself, that one must follow.

> And if it is your new Light leads you on
> To such an admirable gait, for God's sake,
> Follow it, follow it, follow it, Lancelot.

There is tragedy in never seeing the light; the greatest
tragedy, however, consists in seeing it, but refusing to
follow it.

The "Credo" of his first volume remains his strong conviction. His own gleam is poetry.

DEAR FRIENDS

> Dear friends, reproach me not for what I do,
> Nor counsel me, nor pity me; nor say
> That I am wearing half my life away
> For bubble-work that only fools pursue.
> And if my bubbles be too small for you,
> Blow bigger then your own: the games we play
> To fill the frittered minutes of a day,
> Good glasses are to read the spirit through.

And whoso reads may get him some shrewd skill;
And some unprofitable scorn resign,
To praise the very thing that he deplores;
So, friends (dear friends), remember, if you will,
The shame I win for singing is all mine,
The gold I miss for dreaming is all yours.

One cannot question Robinson's fidelity to his gleam.

POETICAL WORKS

THE TOWN DOWN THE RIVER   *Charles Scribner's Sons*

THE CHILDREN OF THE NIGHT   *Charles Scribner's Sons*

CAPTAIN CRAIG   *The Macmillan Company*

THE MAN AGAINST THE SKY
                             The Macmillan Company

MERLIN   *The Macmillan Company*

LANCELOT   *Thomas Seltzer*

AVON'S HARVEST   *The Macmillan Company*

ROMAN BARTHOLOW   *The Macmillan Company*

THE MAN WHO DIED TWICE
                             The Macmillan Company

DIONYSUS IN DOUBT   *The Macmillan Company*

TRISTRAM   *The Macmillan Company*

SONNETS   *The Macmillan Company*

CAVENDER'S HOUSE   *The Macmillan Company*

COLLECTED POEMS   *The Macmillan Company*

CARL SANDBURG

CARL SANDBURG

IN *Who's Who in America,* Carl Sandburg calls himself an "American folk song recitalist"; and thereby —as one is so likely to do in self-analysis—tells only half the story. It is true that in recording the folk songs of America, in putting them into permanent form in his *The American Songbag,* and in singing them to audiences throughout the country, Sandburg is helping to save a past rapidly dying out. It is just as true, and possibly more important, that in writing his own poems of the prairies and of the cities, of nature and of industry, of shy dreamers and of noisy jazz-hounds, he is creating a new body of song that will help perpetuate the America of today, that complex, diversified America which cannot be easily or simply expressed.

It is significant that this poet of the America of today comes from Illinois and not from one of the older Atlantic seaboard states; that he is the son of Swedish immigrants and not the descendant of an old American family. For he himself experienced—he did not inherit—his Americanism; and knowledge that is the result of experience is likely to be vivid and real and very forceful.

At times, it is true, such knowledge may be harsh, and rough, and crude. It is the material of poetry; but before it can become poetry itself, it must be refined, molded, and related. So, while developing his Americanism, Sandburg did not deny his Norse ancestry. From that and from his own instinctive poetic nature came the dreaming, brooding aspect of the man, his desire to look beneath the surface of things for the last reality, the mystic essence of the universe.

These two elements are manifest in his poetry. Some of his poems are loud, raucous, crude; others are tender and gracious. Some of them are sharp, specific, detailed pictures; others are subtle and suggestive intimations of a general truth. At times the two elements are not finely balanced. As one or the other is exaggerated, the result is either a confused catalogue of details or a tenuous idea too vaguely expressed to be understood. But when the two elements merge—when the observer and dreamer, when the doer and thinker, are one—the poet creates his truest poetry.

There was little to suggest the poet in the family or in the early life of Carl Sandburg. His father and mother had come from Sweden to Galesburg in the western part of Illinois, a town with the prairies near at hand. The father, a railroad blacksmith, had been named August Johnson; but he had changed his name to Sandburg because there were so many Johnsons in the company's employ that there were numerous difficulties in receiving one's pay. Neither the elder Sandburg nor his wife had had more than a few weeks' schooling. So for their son, Carl, who was born on January 6, 1878, they did not see the need of an extended formal education. Furthermore, money was scarce in the Sandburg household and Carl's help was needed to supplement the family's income.

Carl, however, did attend school until he was about thirteen. His school days were little different from those of his companions. He studied and applied his learning in writing letters for his father and his neighbors, who could not write. He read—the Rollo books, fairy tales, books of history and of biography. He played ball with the other boys and with them went swimming in the swimming-hole in a deserted brickyard.

When school days were over, there began a series of jobs that brought him into contact with all kinds of people, that enabled him to know their work and their dreams, that gave him an intimate knowledge of the builders of the new America. He drove a milk-wagon in Galesburg. He became a porter in a barber-shop.

"This is where I first got acquainted with the American congressman," he later told Harry Hansen.[1] "A congressman from Galesburg died and about twenty to thirty congressmen and senators from Washington came to bury him. I guess I had the usual kid's exalted view of these men until I blacked their boots." Thereafter, he was not to be awed by a man's official position; it was always the man's inner self in which he was interested. Sandburg's own comment on this story is: "I felt sorry for those congressmen because they had such poor feet."

Then he became, in succession, a scene shifter in a cheap theater, a truck handler in a brickyard, a turner apprentice

[1] Harry Hansen, *Midwest Portraits: A Book of Memories and Friendship*; Harcourt, Brace and Company, New York.

in a pottery. Soon the world beyond Illinois called him. Stealing rides and working his way, he traveled through the West. He was a dishwasher in hotels in Denver, in Omaha, and in Kansas City. He was a harvest hand in Kansas wheatfields. He became a carpenter's helper. He went from house to house, with a pot of blacking in his hands, offering to blacken stoves in exchange for meals.

Somehow, he drifted back to Galesburg. He was learning the painter's trade when, in 1898, the Spanish American war broke out. Sandburg enlisted and served eight months in Company C, 6th Illinois Infantry, the first regiment to set foot in Porto Rico.

One of his fellow soldiers, who was planning to go to college at the expiration of the war, persuaded "Cully" to go, too. So, mustered out from the army with $100 and a determination to acquire learning, Sandburg presented himself at Lombard College, in Galesburg. At the end of his first college year, the officers and men of his military company chose him as a candidate for West Point. He passed physically and mentally in every way at the national military academy—except in arithmetic. He was rejected, and returned to Lombard.

At college, "the terrible Swede" was captain of the basketball team and editor-in-chief of the college monthly and of *The Cannibal*, the college annual. He had to earn his living while he studied. So he became a bell-ringer for the college, gymnasium janitor, and college correspondent for *The Daily Mail*.

Thus college in Sandburg's life was a significant episode, the turning-point of a career. It did not come in the orderly, to-be-expected course of events; it was the result of a conscious and determined decision. It meant the giving up of a life of manual labor for that of a brain worker. Most important, it gave him the means of expressing in terms of literature the impressions he had gathered and the feelings he had experienced in his crowded youth.

Furthermore, in Philip Green Wright, college gave him a helpful friend and adviser. Professor Wright taught English, mathematics, and astronomy. He was a teacher whose vision was not limited by classroom walls.

Recognizing Sandburg's literary ability, he invited him and two other students to form "The Poor Writers' Club," which met in his study on Sunday afternoons. At these meetings, the young men brought for discussion and criticism what they had written during the week. Mr. Wright encouraged Sandburg in his writing, and in 1904 wrote the preface to *In Reckless Ecstasy*, a slender pamphlet of verse and prose, the first printed work of the poet, which was published under the name of Charles A. Sandburg.

Sandburg is said to rejoice in the fact that the issue of *In Reckless Ecstasy* was so small a one that the book is not now likely to come into the hands of many readers. True, the book contains no very great literature. But it is too important for an understanding of the poet's later work to be lightly ignored.

In the first place, consider the title of his book and of its opening article. The phrase "reckless ecstasy," Sandburg says, he got from that romantic writer, Marie Corelli. "There are depths of life," he explains, "that logic cannot sound. It takes feeling. I try to express my-

self sensibly but if that fails I will use the reckless ecstasy
—which may bring home ideas which cannot be stated in
direct words." This manner of suggestion Sandburg was
to employ in his later writing.

In the second place, one should, consider the form in
which the book's poetry was cast—unrhymed, cadenced
verse. Sandburg did not originate such verse; others had
used it before him. But 1904, it must be remembered, was
many years before the rise of the "new poets" and the
concerted efforts of the "new poets" to create new verse
forms. On the other hand, it must not be thought that
Sandburg's method of writing was a haphazard one or
one due to his ignorance of traditional poetic forms. Sandburg had been to college; he had read and was fond of
Keats and Shelley; and he had had literary criticism from
his instructor. It was rather that the rolling, marching
cadences came naturally to him and seemed to him the
most appropriate vehicle for the expression of his thoughts.

Finally, the spirit of the book is important. In it there
is sympathy with human suffering, for the "carryin' in
boys," for example, working out their lives in the glass
factories of Millville. There is a protest against the industrial system that makes possible such labor. In "Pulse
Beats and Pen-Strokes," the criticizer of the social order
rebels and predicts:

> For the hovels shall pass and the shackles drop,
> The gods shall tumble and the system fall.

There is, too, a thrilling sense of his own identity and importance, not conceit but the conception of the place each

man must hold in the universe: "I am the one man in all the world most important to myself." And in "Invocation," there are the requests he makes for himself:

Let me always in my decisions and actions lean rather toward equanimity than ardor. . . .

Make me a good mixer among people, one who always passes along the Good Word. . . .

Constrain me to common sense. . . .

May the potencies of song and laughter abide with me ever.

Whatever theories and hopes about writing Sandburg may have had after he left college, his immediate concern was that of earning a living. For a time he was advertising manager of a department store. In 1904, when his book was published, he was a salesman of stereographs for the New York firm of Underwood and Underwood. On his trips through the small towns in the East, he came to know their men and women as years before he had known the people of the Western towns and farms. All this knowledge, all his wealth of impressions, was later to be transformed into poems.

In this fashion, each of his various positions had its influence on his poetry; in each his keen observation of facts and his quick sympathy with people were called into play, deepened, and enriched. Most of them, moreover, had an even more direct effect; for these called upon his ability as a writer and gave him experience and training in the use of his literary tools.

Sandburg, interested in social well-being and in the political means for obtaining it, was in 1907 and 1908 a district organizer for the Social-Democratic party of Wisconsin. It was in June of this latter year that he married Lillian Steichen, the sister of the photographer; and her sympathy and understanding have encouraged him in all his work. From 1910 to 1912 he was secretary to Mayor Seidel of Milwaukee. At the time of this appointment, he was city hall reporter for the Milwaukee *Journal*.

Then, for a time, he was a member of the editorial staff of *System*, a Chicago magazine of business and industry. His chief interest lay in safety campaigns for workers. In two articles on this subject that he wrote for the magazine, "Muzzling Factory Machines" and "Training Workers to be Careful," one notes his direct handling of facts. It is with vivid and specific instances that he deals, not with vague and theoretical generalizations. One underlying general principle, however, is present: a profound sympathy with the worker and fear lest he become the victim of his machine. Years later he wrote in a letter about *R.U.R.* the play of mechanized men: [2] "That is, any machine, whether robot or flivver or submarine boat or aeroplane, must be watched or it will turn with its curse and revolt against those who make it." The usefulness, the necessity of the machine, even its beauty, no one acknowledges more readily than does Sandburg; but no one is

[2] *New York Times*, January 28, 1923.

quicker to denounce it when it destroys or warps human life.

In 1914 he worked on *The Day Book,* a Chicago daily newspaper that was entirely independent of advertisements. In that year Sandburg first became known to the literary world. *Poetry* published a number of his poems and awarded to his "Chicago" the Helen Haire Levinson Prize of $200 for "the best poem written by a citizen of the United States during the year."

Caustic criticism was hurled at a conception of poetry that would include a poem beginning:

Hog Butcher for the World,
Tool Maker, Stacker of Wheat,
Player with Railroads and the Nation's Freight Handler;
Stormy, husky, brawling
City of the Big Shoulders.

But to its creator it was poetry; and in all his later poems, as in this, Sandburg kept faith with his own poetic ideals.

In 1917 Sandburg joined the staff of the Chicago *Daily News.* Except for a year's connection with the Newspaper Enterprise Association as special correspondent in Sweden and Norway, his work has since been with that newspaper. He has reported labor conventions and news of trade unions; he has served as motion-picture and as literary editor; he has written editorials; he has made notable studies of local problems. His study of the conditions underlying the Chicago race riots of 1918, for example—articles which have been collected and printed in book form—reveal a sound judgment and an amazing reportorial accuracy and fidelity to fact.

This aspect of his intellect is commented upon again and again by those who know him. His mind is a vast storehouse of bits of information. Sherwood Anderson, the writer, tells [3] of an evening when he invited Sandburg to meet a distinguished Frenchman. The two men seemed to have nothing in common; they sat staring at each other. Then Sandburg drew from his pocket papers covered with figures. "So and so many thousand tons of coal," he informed the visitor, "are brought into Chicago each day. It is so many miles from Chicago to Dallas."

The host was in amused despair until he induced Sandburg to go to the piano and sing. "His voice is mellow and rich and he has the gift of song," Anderson writes. "He sang nigger songs, a song of the boll-weevil, one about Jesse James, another about a tough girl of the city streets whose lover had proved unfaithful.

"Sandburg singing, naïvely, beautifully, was something the Frenchman understood and loved."

So there is Sandburg, the reporter; and there is Sandburg, the singer, who before all sorts of audiences sings to his own guitar accompaniment the folk songs that he has gathered in his travels, who explains his theory of poetry, and recites his poems, which are immeasurably enriched by his slow, marvelous voice.

And then there is Sandburg, the creative writer. While busy with his newspaper work, he has written poem after poem. In 1915 appeared his volume *Chicago Poems*, a

[3] "Carl Sandburg," *The Bookman*, December 1921.

book of the city. *Cornhuskers,* 1918, which goes back for its material chiefly to the western Illinois where the poet was born, won for him a share with Margaret Widdemer in the Poetry Society Prize. Again in 1920 he shared this prize, this time with Stephen Vincent Benét, and this time for *Smoke and Steel,* a book of shops and factories and, more than that, a book of human beings. *Slabs of the Sunburnt West* was published in 1922 and in 1928 appeared *Good Morning, America,* in which with stricter discipline increased power and strength seem to have come to the poet. In addition to his poetry, Sandburg has written his Rootabaga stories for children, modern and wholly unconventionalized fairy tales; and, the result of pains-taking and devoted labor, his biography, *Abraham Lincoln: The Prairie Years.*

Sandburg, in his creative work, does not write rapidly. He gets an idea, jots it down in pencil, mulls over it, changes it, types it. In typewritten form he carries it about with him, maybe for a year or for two years, before he has fashioned it to his satisfaction. Much of his work is done in the newspaper room of the *Daily News,* where he frequently taps away at his typewriter until late at night. Some of it is done in the workroom of his home in Elmhurst, a suburb a little way out from Chicago.

Harry Hansen in his *Midwest Portraits* describes this room. "The straw matting on the floor shows signs of use; the little flat-topped desk and the tables may have had several owners; the pine shelves, raised by Carl himself, are there to bear their burden of books, and not to support a scheme of decoration; throughout you get the impression that this is the room of a man without pose, without external furbishing; a man of wide interests and sympathies, as one may deduce from the varied character of Chinese prints, newspaper half-tones, press clippings, pinned about—an old banjo with a string broken; a guitar laid carefully on a bookshelf; a battered suit case. A cot, covered with a Navajo blanket."

He pictures the house itself: "A quaint rambling place it is, a homey place, with many little rooms, cozy and comfortable and without pretense; part of the house was once a little old-fashioned school-house and there is evidence that bits have been added now and then. Mrs. Sandburg is the kindly spirit that hovers over the roof-tree with genial informality, and if you remain long enough three lively youngsters will come romping in, tossing their hats in childish abandon, radiating health and good cheer—Margaret, Janet, and the little curly-headed Helga—you will meet them all in the dedications of several of Carl's books, and again in the poems. They are, as Carl will tell you, with a twinkle, the heirs to the Sandburg millions—millions of clippings."

At one time Sandburg wished to buy additional land for his home. The property owner, selling it, said, "Since it is Mr. Sandburg who is buying it, I won't need a mortgage. His name on a note is good enough for me."

This suggests the nature of Sandburg the man, his honesty, his sincerity, his appeal to other people. A pen-portrait of his external traits would present a tall, rangy, square-shouldered man, with a bit of a stoop, a build suggesting greater physical power than he actually possesses. A cap is pulled down over one eye; long grayish hair falls over his forehead. His weather-beaten face is rugged and rough, with strong jaws and a jutting chin. He does not dress fastidiously, even for formal occasions; sturdy, rough suits, cheap shirts, strong square-built shoes content him. His movements are heavy and slow.

But such a picture is not complete. None is that omits the force of his personality, that fails to suggest the fundamental tenderness and sensitiveness and sympathy of the man. "When he enters a room," says Sherwood Anderson, "every one knows a personage has arrived, but there is no swagger about him." Another writer describes him: [4] "I see him leaning across the table in the little Italian restaurant, the most human, the most intensely alive man I have ever known."

It is from the fusion of all these elements that is evolved Sandburg the poet. And for him, poetry is not something extraneous. "People write poetry because they want to. It functions in them as air in the nostrils of an athlete in a sprint. Moods, thoughts, emotions, surge over writers as they do over inventors and politicians. It is a dark stuff of light that comes and goes." [5]

This last sentence suggests the thirty-eight definitions of poetry that he wrote for the editor of the *Atlantic Monthly* and which have been reprinted in *Good Morning, America*. Two of them provide clews to the fundamental aspects of Sandburg's verse: "Poetry is a series of explanations of life, fading off into horizons too swift for

[4] Paul L. Benjamin, "Poet of the Commonplace," *Survey*, October 2, 1920.
[5] "The Work of Ezra Pound," *Poetry*, February 1916.

explanations." "Poetry is the capture of a picture, a song, or a flair, in a deliberate prism of words."

Thus there are vivid pictures like "Even Numbers" and "Village in Late Summer" and "Hydrangeas":

Dragoons, I tell you the white hydrangeas turn rust and
    go soon.
Already mid September a line of brown runs over them.
One sunset after another tracks the faces, the petals.
Waiting, they look over the fence for what way they go.

And there are those other poems, "explanations of life," that give suggestions and hints from which the reader may build up truths. In "Limited," for example, consider the delicacy, combined with force and irony, with which the poet suggests man's passage through this life:

I am riding on a limited express, one of the crack trains
    of the nation.
Hurtling across the prairie into blue haze and dark air go
    fifteen all-steel coaches holding a thousand people.
(All the coaches shall be scrap and rust and all the men
    and women laughing in the diners and sleepers shall
    pass to ashes.)
I ask a man in the smoker where he is going and he
    answers: "Omaha."

Within his definition of poetry come every phase of American life, every activity, every object. Sandburg finds poetry where others have found it and in addition creates it where none has seen it before. He sees—and conveys to others—the poetry of the broad sweep of the prairies, of the song of the frogs, of skyscrapers, of motor cars, and the "new farm tractor," of jazz and the winds, and the sea, of stockyards, of the "yellow dust on a bumblebee's wings," of Kubelik, and a hangman, of a telephone operator, and Emily Dickinson, and a "fish crier":

His face is that of a man terribly glad to be selling fish,
    terribly glad that God made fish, and customers to
    whom he may call his wares from a pushcart.

Just as the subject matter of Sandburg's poetry is comprehensive, embracing all phases of the America of today, so is his language inclusive, vibrant, alive. "Unless we keep on the lookout," he says, "we write book language and employ the verbiage of dead men instead of using the speech of people alive today." Gone, then, are worn-out words and phrases trailing shreds of old poetic value. They have been made to give up their place to a new poetic diction expressive of a modern world; they have yielded to the speech of the man-in-the-street, even to his slang. "Monicker," "do a fadeaway," "harness bulls," "dicks," "croaked," "necktie party"—these are a random few, indicative of what may be found throughout Sandburg's work.

The practice of such a theory of poetry has its inherent defects. It limits the poetry's appeal in time and in place. Slang, after all, has a brief life; and nothing is quite so woebegone as a slang phrase passed out of current use. The slang of one class of people is quite without meaning to people of other classes, the slang of one community unintelligible to others. Something of the bewilderment that this poetry can cause is reflected in a review in the English *Westminster Gazette.*

"Without Miss Rebecca West's illuminating picture of Chicago in the preface, many of the *Selected Poems of Carl Sandburg* would be meaningless to the average English reader, so packed are his verses with strange words and phrases, alien to our genius and our language."

These limitations must be recognized and overcome by the poet. As for the critic, he cannot dismiss the poems simply because their method or language is new. The working out of a new technique is a poet's privilege and right.

In an interview [6] Sandburg once said, "There are a group of us in the United States—perhaps you'd call us a type—who are struggling along after a kind of freedom. We are not sure we are writing poetry—I guess really we don't know where we're going, but we're on our way."

That way is a progressive one. Rules of poetry are simply evolved out of the practice of the past; they should not be permitted to restrain new attempts in the present. That they can be modified is shown by the attitude toward cadenced verse. When Sandburg first wrote, he had to defend and champion its use for poetry; now, it is calmly accepted as one of the recognized forms.

This same liberalizing effect is found in his diction. Whatever the conflicting opinions may be concerning the use of slang, it cannot be denied that Sandburg has given

[6] Walter Yust, "Carl Sandburg, Human Being," *The Bookman,* January 1921.

poetic value to words that heretofore have not possessed it. Consider his use of proper nouns, as in "Localities," for example:

Wagon Wheel Gap is a place I never saw
And Red Horse Gulch and the chutes of Cripple Creek.
Red-shirted miners picking in the sluices,
Gamblers with red neckties in the night streets,
The fly-by-night towns of Bull Frog and Skiddoo,
The night-cool limestone white of Death Valley,
The straight drop of eight hundred feet
From a shelf road in the Hasiampa Valley:
Men and places they are I never saw.

When one accepts the principle that any word fittingly used may be a poetical word, the next problem is that of choice: which word is the most suitable, the most forceful? In his poem "Basket" Sandburg has suggested the necessity of selection:

Speak, sir, and be wise.
Speak choosing your words, sir, like an old woman over a
    bushel of apples.

One of his own principles of selection is this: "I cut out all words ending in *ity* and *ness* as far as I can. That is, I cut out words describing 'state of being.' And I search for the picture-words, as the Indians have them, as the Chinese have them."

The result of this selective process is a kaleidoscopic parade of pictures. Image after image is vividly presented, sharp, clear, indelible. Their value is strengthened by

Sandburg's rich use of figures, his ability to see compari-
sons and fix them. A house to him is "empty as a beggar's
tin cup on a rainy day, empty as a soldier's sleeve with
an arm lost." For him dawn does not break; rather he sees
"the night slur into dawn." And at sunset,

> Night gathers itself into a ball of dark yarn,
> Night loosens the ball and it spreads.

One of the developments of this use of figures is that
of symbolism. An idea is expressed not directly, in its
own terms, but in terms of an extended comparison. Hats,
for example, become symbols of their wearers: "Hats have
a destiny; wish your hat slowly; your hat is you." A more
striking example is "Clean Curtains," wherein the white
curtains at the windows of a house, curtains like the "rim
of a nun's bonnet," are made to reflect a family's unsuccessful efforts to withstand the force of a demoralizing
environment.

To make his impressions still more vivid, Sandburg
frequently uses repetition. Words and phrases run like a
refrain through his poems, holding parts together, deep-
ening the effect of the whole. The repeated "huddled and
ugly walls" sets the tone of "The Harbor." So, too, the
devotion of husband and wife in "A Couple" is sounded
through the reiterated:

> "The crying is lonely," she wrote him.
> "The same here," he answered.

And in "Southern Pacific" the whole poem is built up of
repetition.

SOUTHERN PACIFIC

Huntington sleeps in a house six feet long.
Huntington dreams of railroads he built and owned.
Huntington dreams of ten thousand men saying: Yes, sir.

Blithery sleeps in a house six feet long.
Blithery dreams of rails and ties he laid.
Blithery dreams of saying to Huntington: Yes, sir.

Huntington,
Blithery, sleep in houses six feet long.

In this poem the effect gained by repetition cannot be divorced from that gained by contrast. As the title of his volume *Smoke and Steel* suggests, Sandburg delights in this device. His poems abound with the differences between man and nature, between rich and poor, as in "Graceland" and in "The Right to Grief," between worker and idler, and—symbolically—between night and day.

FIVE TOWNS ON THE B. AND O.

By day—tireless smokestacks—hungry smoky shanties hanging to the slopes—crooning: We get by, that's all.
By night—all lit up—fire-gold bars, fire-gold flues—and the shanties shaking in clumsy shadows—almost the hills shaking—all crooning: By God, we're going to find out or know why.

These technical devices of rhythm, diction, imagery, repetition, and contrast—to what use are they put by Sandburg? His purpose is to express the America he knows, its whole broad sweep, not one small corner of it, nor yet its reflection in the personality of a single one of its citizens. So vast and complicated a subject, if it is to be treated as a single entity, must be handled in a large, panoramic, epic manner. This is his method in "Prairie":

Here the water went down, the icebergs slid with gravel, the gaps and the valleys hissed, and the black loam came, and the yellow sandy loam.

Here between the shed of the Rocky Mountains and the Appalachians, here now a morning star fixes a fire sign over the timber claims and cow pastures, the corn belt, the cotton belt, the cattle ranches.

Here the gray geese go five hundred miles and back with a wind under their wings honking the cry for a new home.

Here I know I will hanker after nothing so much as one more sunrise or a sky moon of fire doubled to a river moon of water.

> .   .   .   .

I speak of new cities and new people.

I tell you the past is a bucket of ashes.

I tell you yesterday is a wind gone down, a sun dropped in the west.

I tell you there is nothing in the world only an ocean of tomorrows, a sky of tomorrows.

I am a brother of the cornhuskers who say at sundown:

Tomorrow is a day.

It is his method, too, in his treatment of a city, as in "The Sins of Kalamazoo" and in "Chicago" and its elaboration, "The Windy City." The history of the city is suggested, pictures of its buildings are sketched, snapshots of its people presented, and a glimpse given of its soul:

> Winds of the Windy City,
> Winds of corn and sea blue,
> Spring wind white and fighting winter gray,
> Come home here—they nickname a city for you.
> The wind of the lake shore waits and wanders.
> The heave of the shore wind hunches the sand piles.
> The winkers of the morning stars count out cities
> And forget the numbers.

And again, on a still larger scale, molding prairie and city into one, he sings the song of a whole nation in "Good Morning, America," The Harvard Phi Beta Kappa poem for 1928. America is seen developing through war and industry from its first colonial beginnings to its present position of importance: "Now it's Uncle Sam sitting on top of the world." What has happened to other civilizations? They have crumbled and disappeared:

> Morning goes as morning-glories go!
> High noon goes, afternoon goes!
> Twilight, sundown, gloaming—
> The hour of writing: Good night, America!
> Good night, sleep, peace, and sweet dreams!
>   .   .   .   .
> The prints of many new ships shall be on the sky.
> The Four Horsemen shall ride again in a bitter dust,

The granaries of great nations shall be the food of fat rats,
And the shooting stars shall write new alphabets on the
      sky
   Before we come home,
   Before we understand.

What, then, can he ask for America? Though its material wealth may vanish, that its beauty and dreams and
soul remain:

Sea sunsets, give us keepsakes.
Prairie gloamings, pay us for prayers.
Mountain clouds on bronze skies—
   Give us great memories.
Let us have summer roses.
Let us have tawny harvest haze in pumpkin time.
Let us have spring time faces to toil for and play for.
Let us have the fun of booming winds on long waters.
Give us dreamy blue twilights—of winter evenings—to
      wrap us in a coat of dreaminess.
Moonlight, come down—shine down, moonlight—meet
      every bird cry and every song calling to a hard old
      earth, a sweet young earth.

An examination of these long poems reveals that
though they are vast and sweeping in effect, in method
they are lyrical. They are made up of a series of gleams,
a number of small, compact episodes. Such, for example,
are the sketches of the men of colonial times and of the
soldiers of the great war in the last poem.
   One realizes the infinite variety of the component parts

of these poems and of the component parts of their mighty subject. And because Sandburg's shorter poems are no less expressive of America, one realizes that these, too, will vary—vary in mood, in tone, and in subject.

The mood of Sandburg's poems ranges from the surly indignation of "You take your grief and I mine—see?" through the sheer joy of life in "Potato Blossom Songs":

Rum tiddy um
Tiddy um
Tiddy um tum tum
My knees are loose-like, my feet want to sling their selves.
I feel like tickling you under the chin—honey—and
    a-asking: Why Does a Chicken Cross the Road?

At times he speaks in loud, harsh tones. But he does so only when his subject demands it. The modulations of his voice within a single poem, modulations to suit his material, are shown in "Knucks," when brass knuckles are found in Mister Fischman's store in "Lincoln's City." A voice that can be stridently loud becomes gently crooning in "Fog":

The fog comes
on little cat feet.

It sits looking
over harbor and city
on silent haunches
and then moves on.

This is the voice that he uses for that large number of poems which might best be called lyrics of personal emotion. Underlying them are those fundamental qualities of Sandburg himself, gentleness and love. "Baby Song of the Four Winds" is typical of these. So, too, is the hauntingly beautiful "The Great Hunt":

> I cannot tell you now;
>   When the wind's drive and whirl
>   Blow me along no longer,
>   And the wind's a whisper at last—
> Maybe I'll tell you then—
>   some other time.
>
>   When the rose's flash to the sunset
>   Reels to the rack and the twist,
>   And the rose is a red bygone,
>   When the face I love is going
>   And the gate to the end shall clang,
>   And it's no use to beckon or say, "So long"—
> Maybe I'll tell you then—
>   some other time.
>
> I never knew any more beautiful than you;
>   I have hunted you under my thoughts,
>   I have broken down under the wind
>   And into the rose looking for you.
>   I shall never find any
>   greater than you.

In contrast with these are his poems of social significance. Prompted by his profound human sympathy, he must protest against the evils of our civilization. Some-

times he uses satire, but it is seldom personal. Nor does
he ever show any vindictiveness. And rarely, it must be
admitted, does he offer any solution. Most frequently,
his protests take the form of simple statements of conditions.

His earlier war poems are simply pictures. The dying
soldier of "Murmurings in a Field Hospital," who longs
for "only beautiful useless things," is just one of those

> Sixteen million men
> Chosen for shining teeth,
> Sharp eyes, hard legs
> And a running of young warm blood in their wrists

against whose fate Sandburg is indignant. It is the waste
of war, its futility, that concerns him, as in "Buttons":

Who would guess what it cost to move two buttons one
   inch on the war map there in front of the newspaper
   office where the freckled-faced young man is laugh-
   ing to us.

Relief from war's tragedies can come only with for-
getfulness.

A. E. F.

There will be a rusty gun on the wall, sweetheart,
The rifle grooves curling with flakes of rust.
A spider will make a silver string nest in the darkest,
   warmest corner of it.
The trigger and the range-finder, they too will be rusty.

And no hands will polish the gun, and it will hang on the
    wall.
Forefingers and thumbs will point absently and casually
    toward it.
It will be spoken among half-forgotten, wished-to-be-
    forgotten things.
They will tell the spider: Go on, you're doing good work.

It is with unwonted bitterness that he finally sums up his
antagonism to war in "And So Today."

> The boy nobody knows the name of—
> The buck private—the unknown soldier—
> The doughboy who dug under and died
> When they told him to—that's him.

While this honored—and sacrificed—victim is being
buried, a skeleton army of other dead rides by and asks,
"Why?"

There is the same sort of protest against some of the
results of industrialism. There are vivid pictures of workers in "The Mayor of Gary," in "Onion Days"; criticism
of child labor in "They Will Say"; of improper work
conditions in "Anna Imroth." His sympathies are aroused
—sometimes to the point of sentimentality—not by poverty so much as by unremitting toil that makes men

> Tired of wishes,
> Empty of dreams.

His wish for man is for "some rag of romance, some
slant of a scarlet star."

CARL SANDBURG

That riches are not necessary for romance and for happiness he well knows. In "Happiness" he finds true happiness not with professors or "famous executives" but in a "crowd of Hungarians under the trees with their women and children and a keg of beer and an accordion." And in "Fellow Citizens" a maker of musical instruments "had it all over" Chicago's millionaires and politicians:

.Anyway he is the only Chicago citizen
I was jealous of that day.

Here it must be repeated that it is not labor of itself that Sandburg condemns. No one knows better than he that work is essential to happiness. None more than he glories in the creation of man's labor. He is, without doubt, the most sincere exalter of man-made cities, cities of skyscrapers and moonlight, of dancers, of noise, of people and work and life.

PRAYERS OF STEEL

Lay me on an anvil, O God,
Beat me and hammer me into a crowbar.
Let me pry loose old walls.
Let me lift and loosen old foundations.

Lay me on an anvil, O God,
Beat me and hammer me into a steelspike.
Drive me into the girders that hold a skyscraper together.
Take red-hot rivets and fasten me into the central girders.
Let me be the great nail holding a skyscraper through
    blue nights into white stars.

But how can he reconcile his two views, his glory in labor, in machines, and in larger masses with his pity for their exhausted products? He offers no solution, except the solution of a democracy in which each man's worth is recognized, each man's place in the universe acknowledged. And to him the all-embracing democracy is death:

COOL TOMBS

When Abraham Lincoln was shoveled into the tombs, he forgot the copperheads and the assassin—in the dust, in the cool tombs.

And Ulysses Grant lost all thought of con men and Wall Street, cash and collateral turned ashes—in the dust, in the cool tombs.

Pocahontas' body, lovely as a poplar, sweet as a red haw in November or a paw paw in May, did she wonder? does she remember?—in the dust, in the cool tombs?

Take any streetful of people buying clothes and groceries, cheering a hero or throwing confetti and blowing tin horns—tell me if the lovers are losers—tell me if any get more than the lovers—in the dust—in the cool tombs.

But since death comes to all, it is not to be considered a cruel termination:

Death is a nurse mother with big arms: "I won't hurt you at all; it's your time now; you just need a long sleep, child; what have you had anyhow better than sleep?"

This gentleness of death, its appropriate place in the scheme of things, is a fundamental conviction of Sandburg's. For he believes in the essential rightness of the universe. The search for the ultimate reality may be a blind wild groping because of the imperfections of the senses, as he suggests in "Slabs of the Sunburnt West." But there is a faith beyond the senses, a mystic awareness that all is right:

CABOOSE THOUGHTS

It's going to come out all right—do you know?
The sun, the birds, the grass—they know,
They get along—and we'll get along.

This faith is more than a personal one. It is the faith of America itself, of a country made up of cities and prairies, winds and mists, tawny sun and hazy moonlight, hollyhocks and skyscrapers, work and play, noises and silences, life and death. Because Sandburg in his own life has touched this America at so many points, he can sing its faith and soul with no small degree of assurance and of authority. Though his own personality colors all his poems, it is this larger personality that he succeeds in expressing. Sandburg becomes, then, the poet of America. Something more than the modest recitalist that he calls himself, he becomes the creator of a new body of American folk song.

POETICAL WORKS

CHICAGO POEMS   *Henry Holt and Co.*

CORNHUSKERS   *Henry Holt and Co.*

SMOKE AND STEEL   *Harcourt, Brace and Company*

SLABS OF THE SUNBURNT WEST
                   Harcourt, Brace and Company

SELECTED POEMS   *Harcourt, Brace and Company*

GOOD MORNING, AMERICA
                   Harcourt, Brace and Company

WALTER DE LA MARE

WALTER DE LA MARE

"TO ME, of course," Walter de la Mare once said,[1] "it is utter nonsense to assume that an imaginative piece of poetry is lacking in reality. An imaginative experience is not only as real but far realer than an unimaginative one."

That statement holds the key to De la Mare's poetry. It unlocks for the reader what might be the otherwise puzzling question of the poetry's subject matter, its dream and fantasy content, and of its childlike and elusive attitude toward the world which grown-ups call real.

Possibly to no one more than to a child does the imagined seem as real as the unimagined. For him dreams and fairies and ghosts have all the actuality that family and business, love and work and religion, have for an adult; they make the same demands and require the same adjustments of conduct. Moreover, they provide a haven of escape and comfort from the misunderstandings and cruelties of a non-child world. In a poet, then, who has retained childhood's ability to make dreams seem real, it is not surprising to find in addition to poems written directly for children, other poems, written for grown-up

[1] Virginia Rice, "On not Interviewing Walter de la Mare," *The Bookman*, September 1922.

children, that utilize the symbols of a child, that manifest a child's sense of awe and curiosity, and that give to the riddle of the universe a child's answer of a world of make-believe.

The world of fancy is essentially a personal one that none can enter and freely travel save its creator himself. The essence of its truth lies in individual imagination. So, too, the imagination of the individual colors and absorbs the elements of the world about him. "Beauty itself," says De la Mare, "depends for its being less on that which reveals it than on him who perceives it."

It has ever been the function of the poet to crystallize some of this perception of beauty and to share it with others as best he can. For De la Mare this must be a very subjective task, suggesting feelings rather than hoping to re-create an objective fact. In an early review, "An Elizabethan Poet and Modern Poetry," he thus defines his purpose: "To express his love, desire, dream, grief, or rapture, his sense of an age-long solitude beset by a cloud of witnesses, to bear record, if it may be, for a little longer than mortal life permits, to his experience of a strange, absorbing, baffling world, in the briefest and loveliest terms within his power—this alone is every true poet's aim."

Words, however, cannot definitely and completely reveal impressions and emotions; they can, at best, give hints and suggestions. Particularly is this true of imaginative and fancied experience. The dreamer finds it difficult to translate the wonders of his dreams into words satisfactory to himself. It becomes much more difficult, almost impossible, to find words to convey his dreams to others.

In spite of this insistence upon the childlike and fanci-
ful aspect of his verse, De la Mare must not be thought
of as the conventional visionary and dreamer, secluded
and aloof. Walter Tittle in his "Portraits in Pencil and
Pen," in *The Century*, May 1923, describes him as the
center of an animated family group. He is a "dark man
of medium height, with olive skin and eager, sparkling,
black eyes. His black, moderately short hair seemed re-
belliously to declare its independence over the taming
efforts of comb and brush, breaking into triumphant curls
at the front. The spirit of his hair seemed typical of the
man, for the smile that came often and easily made me
think that the small boy within him was always eager to
break the bonds of maturity. Here surely was the ring-
leader of all his children's romping, and well could I
picture him writing his first poems for their amusement.
Here was a poet of inquisitive, exuberant normality, without the eccentricities usually attributed to his kind."

Again, in R. L. Mégroz's study, *Walter de la Mare*,[2]
is the same suggestion that conventional conceptions must
be discarded: "He strode into the room with the gait of
a sailor, the figure of a yeoman, and a strong, mobile face
irradiated with his smile. Some old tweed suit he wore
suggested at once negligence about dress and sufficient
respect for the social proprieties. His high, knotted, and
domed brow, partly concealed by the short, rather ragged,
hair, and his solid-looking head, perhaps fortified the impression he conveyed of a hard-thinking scientist taking a
brief social recreation."

[2] R. L. Mégroz, *Walter de la Mare*, George H. Doran Co., New York.

He has a delightful home life, with his wife and two sons and two daughters. He has a large number of interesting and stimulating friends. His contacts with people are touched and brightened by a kindly humor and an unfailing courtesy and charm. Nor are these the easy graces of a carefree, idyllic life. For a number of years De la Mare knew the exigencies of business in London's "City."

Yet, despite his social grace, his contact with men and women, there is in the poet an essential aloneness, a natural reticence. Those who visit him to interview him usually find themselves the interviewed. He shuns publicity. His life has been uneventful, he would say; there is little about it to tell.

This uneventful life, that possibly found in dreams a substitute for exciting adventure, began on April 25, 1873, in the little village of Charlton in Kent. The boy's father, James Edward, was a churchwarden and the brother of a clergyman; he was of Huguenot extraction, tracing his descent from Jean Baptiste Delamare, who came to England from France in the early eighteenth century. His mother was Lucy Sophia, the daughter of Dr. Colin Arrot Browning. Dr. Browning was a naval surgeon at Woolwich Dockyard, who in his active sea life had been instrumental in reforming the treatment of passengers on Australia-bound convict ships. His accounts of his treatment of convicts were published in two books: *England's Exiles*, 1842, and *The Convict Ship*, 1843. Mr. Mégroz, who brings to light these facts, suggests that there is a not distant relationship between Dr. Browning and Robert Browning, the poet.

Whether his grandfather's writings had any effect upon the young Walter John, or whether the poetry of his more distant kinsman influenced him, one cannot say. As a matter of fact, there is available but little material concerning the boy's early life. It is known, however, that books early played a part in it. The poet himself tells [3] of the world opened to him by *Gulliver's Travels*. "But I can very clearly descry—in a vague spectral fashion can even again become—the small boy of six or seven I then was. He is sitting up in bed, his wits still fringed with dream, and in the folds of his counterpane lie an orange, a red-cheeked apple, a threepenny bit, and a limp stocking that has well served Santa Claus's purpose. It is not, however, the orange or the apple or the threepenny bit that incarnadines the occasion, but a book; a limp, broad picturebook, printed in bold type, with half a dozen or so full-page plates in the primary colors— Gulliver, pinned down by lank strands of his hair and being dragged along by a team of cart-horses, fifty strong, on a vast shallow dray with wheels like reels of cotton; Gulliver entertaining (and being richly entertained by) two sneezing Lilliputians in his gold snuff box; Gulliver with desperate head just emerging from a Brobdingnagian bowl of cream. . . .

"*Gulliver's Travels*, then, was that small boy's first rememberable book. In that minute the most insidious of life's habits had taken this innocent in its nets; the ichor of fantasy had begun to thin his blood. He had become

[3] "Books and Reading," *Saturday Westminster Gazette*, reprinted in *The Living Age*, March 22, 1919.

—and will probably remain to his last hour—the slave of the printed word."

The fascination of the printed word soon manifested itself in a desire to write and to publish. The boy was sent to St. Paul's Cathedral School in London, a school of about forty pupils. There in September 1889, when he was sixteen, he founded *The Choristers' Journal*, the school paper that is still flourishing. It began as a weekly, its copies run off in some unprofessional fashion. Much of the work was done by De la Mare: a question and answer column, editorials, and stories signed W. J. D. Mr. Mégroz in his book quotes an article on girls which the future poet wrote:

"A girl always pretends she thinks boys utterly below her in everything. She also thinks that a boy is not worth speaking to but is only meant to assist her in every possible way, but girls have some good qualities for all that, for most of them are generous and very nice when you have trouble to confide in. Of course now I'm speaking mostly of a sister for, of course, I haven't said much about a girl who is not a sister for I have not yet had much experience (of sweethearts, which no doubt are very nice, indeed) but I think that girls especially if they are pretty are not so very bad on the whole. (W. J. D.)"

Books, girls, and stamps! For in several advertisements appearing in *The Choristers' Journal*, attention is called to the extraordinary stamp collection of one De la Mare and of his willingness to sell and exchange. Surely stamps, marked with the names of strange and distant countries, offered rich suggestions to a developing imagination!

After a few months *The Choristers' Journal* announced a change of policy; it was to be formally printed and to come out as a monthly. But the first number to appear in the new form, the issue of April 1890, carried the announcement of De la Mare's departure from school.

The cause of the sudden ending of his schooling is not known. It was not poor scholarship, for De la Mare had for several terms been leading his class. But whatever may have been the reasons for it, is it too much to see in the swift change from school to business an explanation of De la Mare's poetic tendency; a desire to cling to as many joys of childhood as he could, even though they were the joys of fancy; an eagerness to find in dreams a compensation for what must have been the first difficulties of business?

For immediately upon leaving school, at the age of seventeen, he began to work for the Anglo-American Oil Company, the English branch of the Standard Oil Company of America. For eighteen years he worked for this company, the larger part of the time in the statistical department. One wonders what columns of figures meant to the young man. He himself says concerning this period of his life, "I think that one can find an interest in any task which has *got* to be done."

However satisfactory his work was, and it must have been satisfactory to have kept him there for so long a time, his whole interest did not lie in his task. For he began to write stories and poems; and he planned a magazine to be circulated among the staff of the company. There were but two issues, each bound in an artistic cover of brown paper

and costing sixpence; and of these two issues, De la Mare
was editor, publisher, and major contributor. His literary
interests evidently carried over into his appearance. In
an article, "Walter de la Mare as an Editor," appearing
in *The Living Age* for March 27, 1926, and reprinted
from *T.P.'s and Cassell's Weekly*, an unnamed writer thus
describes him:

"The De la Mare of those days not only wrote poetry,
but looked the poet. In a period when the City clerk nearly
choked himself in his high collar and wore his hair close-
clipped, De la Mare affected a low turndown collar with
a flowing black bow of the type associated with French
students in the Latin Quarter. His abundant wavy hair
flowed over his neck in hirsute waves. His headgear was of
the black wide-awake character with a broad flat brim
which is still favored in Chelsea."

The literary promise of his appearance was fulfilled.
In 1895, five years after he had left school, he had his
first story published in *The Sketch*, a macabre tale called
"Kismet." It appeared under the name Walter Ramal,
an anagram of his own name and one that he was to use
for a number of years.

In 1896 the *Cornhill Magazine*, under the editorship
of St. Loe Strachey, began to publish his work. The editor
records his delight at his reading of the first De la Mare
manuscript. This had been brought to his attention by
Roger Ingpen, the writer, whose sister Elfrida had married De la Mare.

From this time on, De la Mare's work appeared regularly in the periodicals. Meantime, he was writing poems

for the pleasure of his own children, poems which he collected and called *Songs of Childhood*. This appeared in 1901, through the instrumentality of Andrew Lang, then acting as reader for the publishing firm of Longmans, Green and Company; and it was Lang who gave it an enthusiastic review in *Longman's Magazine* for March 1902.

In 1904 appeared *Henry Brocken*, the story of a boy's adventures in lands peopled by characters from literature. In 1906 appeared a second volume of verse, called simply *Poems*.

Finally, in 1908 De la Mare left his business office to devote himself completely to his writing. Through the Asquith Government he had been given a small grant and then had later been put on the Civil List with a pension of £100 a year. This sum, together with what he earned by reviewing for *The Saturday Westminster*, *Bookman*, and *Times Literary Supplement*, gave him necessary freedom for his desired writing.

His books appeared now with some frequency; a novel, *The Return*; a children's story, *The Three Mulla Mulgars*; two books of verse for children, *A Child's Day*, 1912, and *Peacock Pie*, 1913; and a third volume of verse, *Listeners*, 1912.

In 1916 *Listeners* appeared in an American edition. The first of his books to be published in this country, it was well received by discerning critics.

In that same year, De la Mare himself came to America. He had been a close friend of Rupert Brooke, the English poet killed in the World War. Brooke, in his

will, had left his money and the proceeds of his books
to be divided among three of his poet friends, Lascelles
Abercrombie, Wilfrid Wilson Gibson, and De la Mare:
"If I can set them free to any extent to write the poetry
and plays and books they want to, my death will bring
more gain than loss." To Brooke, Yale had awarded the
Howland Memorial Prize, and Mrs. Brooke had asked
De la Mare to represent her, come to this country, and
accept it formally.

De la Mare himself tells a story of his visit here. He
had gone to pay a call on a friend of Brooke. "The colored
lift girl inquired who the caller was. I told her. Where-
upon she exclaimed with a smile all radiant gold and ivory,
'Gee whiz! what a name!' "

The gentle humor of this sort that permits him to laugh
at himself is typical of his work. The story, moreover, is
illustrative of his modesty, for he told it to suggest how
little he was known.

But whether or not his name was to become more familiar to elevator operators with each succeeding book,
he was to become better known and more securely established for a growing number of readers. His earlier volumes were reprinted by his American publishers; a play,
books of short stories, and an anthology compiled by him
were printed. He wrote poems to accompany the pictures
of the young artist Pamela Bianco, and three volumes of
poetry, *Motley*, 1918; *The Veil*, 1922; and *Stuff and
Nonsense*, 1927. In addition to several collections of his
poetry, one other book was published, *Memoirs of a
Midget*, 1921. This is noteworthy, for the delicate prose

WALTER DE LA MARE

story established his reputation as a thing beyond question.

It was, moreover, his reputation as a poet that was thus made more secure. For with De la Mare there is a merging of prose and poetry; his two kinds of writing show the same tendencies. He declares that no subject is intended especially for prose or for poetry; the vehicle of expression depends solely upon the writer.

It may be noted that the recognized position which the poet finally achieved was somewhat late in being acknowledged; his popularity did not come at the very beginning of his career. For one thing, De la Mare wrote and published quietly; noisy pressure was not applied to bringing him to popular notice. For another thing, this poet seems to be of the opinion that popular approval is not necessarily the highest or most desired approval; that the best in art is not for the many. This attitude can best be understood in the light of his belief that true beauty lies in the eyes of the beholder.

We "discover the gifts of art," he says, "only by a comparison of what is ours already." Childhood is the common experience of mankind and so it is natural that the poetry of childhood should have a wide appeal. Details of childhood experience vary—and vary widely—according to time and race and class. But of the usual, by no means out of the ordinary, routine of a child's life, De la Mare has made a delightful poem in A Child's Day. The poem tells the story of Elizabeth Ann from the time she wakens and bathes until at night she

> Slips from dressedupedness
> Into her bare,

puts on her night clothes, and goes to bed.

Such simple incidents of a child's life, the vague questioning, the tentative thoughts, become the material of his poetry.

> How large unto the tiny fly
> Must little things appear!

he says in his poem, "The Fly"; and for the purposes of much of his poetry, he assumes the eyes of a fly and makes the things he sees not trivialities but fit subject for poetry. So there is a poem about the child who can't "abear a butcher," and one about Jemima, whose sister, jealous of her bright hair, mockingly calls "Mima, Mima"; and one about the Bandog,

> And he answers to the simple name of Mopser,
> When civilly addressed.

The child of his poetry is not frequently one of a group of children, enjoying noisy games and riotous adventures. He is more likely to be like the child of "Myself":

> And I am there alone:
> Forlornly, silently,
> Plays in the evening garden
> Myself with me.

The child of the evening garden indulges in philosophical musings. Like all abstract thinkers, he realizes his loneliness in this world, the indifference—the unawareness—of others to his existence. He looks out from his window upon people passing; but—

> They cannot see my little room,
>   All yellowed with the shaded sun;
> They do not even know I am here;
>   Nor will guess when I am gone.

How does he console himself for the natural tinge of sorrow that follows such realization? With thoughts of the fairies that dance in a ring, or whirl as flakes of snow; with visions of witches that turn into bushes; with glimpses of a beckoning world, where Pan calls and Queen Djenira slumbers, a world of children whom "magic hath stolen away."

These poems are not written with the tongue-in-cheek, superior attitude of an adult, smilingly and a little patronizingly watching a child. It is the child himself who talks, who has the same acceptance for both the real and the fancied, who as in "Alas! Alack!" hears a fish that *talks* in the sizzling frying-pan; who in "Sam" feels nothing incongruous in hearing his father snore in a world of mermaids and wee folk. As a matter of fact, the child who is living in dream or in fantasy never errs by slipping back into a prosaic world. In "Tartary," details are enumerated with all the verisimilitude of reality:

> If I were Lord of Tartary,
>   Myself and me alone,
> My bed should be of ivory,
>   Of beaten gold my throne;

And in my court would peacocks flaunt,
And in my forests tigers haunt,
And in my pools great fishes slant
    Their fins athwart the sun.

There is earnest seriousness here, as there is in "The Massacre":

The shadow of a poplar tree
    Lay in that lake of sun,
As I with my little sword went in—
    Against a thousand, one.

The attitude of childhood, De la Mare insists, should be retained. It is through the faith of a child that the soul knows victory, he says in "Keep Innocency":

Like an old battle, youth is wild
With bugle and spear, and countercry,
Fanfare and drummery, yet a child
Dreaming of that sweet chivalry,
The piercing terror cannot see. . . .
        .   .   .   .   .
And when the wheeling rout is spent,
Though in the heaps of slain he lie;
Or lonely in his last content;
Quenchless shall burn in secrecy
The flame Death knows his victors by.

When, however, childlike faith fails him, the grown-up De la Mare still escapes as a child escapes. He retreats into a world his fancy creates, a place of twilight, of shadows, of loveliness. In that world there is a memory of the perfections he has once known and from which he feels himself exiled:

EXILE

Had the gods loved me I had lain
    Where darnel is, and thorn,
And the wild night-bird's night-long strain
    Trembles in boughs forlorn.

Nay, but they loved me not; and I
    Must needs a stranger be,
Whose every exiled day gone by
    Aches with their memory.

In it, too, is the longing for the perfections which his dreams imagine.

These dreams of De la Mare are never nightmares! They have the topsy-turvy qualities of dreams, as in "The Thief at Robin's Castle," wherein the thief enjoys his stolen gains as no moral thief should; but there is no sense of maddening and incomprehensible confusion. They are clouded over with an effect of melancholy; but they are not gloomy. The dark, silent houses, even those with friendless faces peering from windows, do not terrify; the ogres and ghosts do not frighten. It is rather that there is present a vague sense of tremulous beauty, "the ghost of that beautiful lady" of "The Three Cherry Trees," the magic silence of "The Sunken Garden":

Speak not—whisper not;
Here bloweth thyme and bergamot;

Softly on the evening hour,
Secret herbs their spices shower.
Dark-spiked rosemary and myrrh,
Lean-stalked, purple lavender;
Hides within her bosom, too,
All her sorrows, bitter rue.

The tone and mood of a poem are never definite statements, never clearly drawn presentations to the reader's intellect; they are, rather, subtle suggestions made to the feelings and emotions. The reader, from within himself, from his own sensitivity, from his own experience and hopes and dreams, must respond to the poem. With almost mystic intuition he will comprehend; the poem's meaning, while shadowy, will never be doubtful. There is this suggestive method of creating atmosphere in "The Sleeper," and in the very well-known "The Listeners":

But only a host of phantom listeners
    That dwelt in the lone house then
Stood listening in the quiet of the moonlight
    To that voice from the world of men.

In much the same manner De la Mare suggests a story rather than tells it in detail. True, in poems like "Sam's Three Wishes" or "Off the Ground," the tale may be told in the more conventional way; but his more usual method is that of "Mistress Fell" and of "The Mocking Fairy," in which but faint suggestions are given from which the reader may create his own story, highly satisfactory to himself.

The atmosphere, then, of De la Mare's poems is that

of his own Tishnar, "that which cannot be thought about
in words or told, or expressed." How are his effects
achieved?

In the first place, he does not hesitate to use words and
expressions that are frankly poetic, and that, because of
their poetic association, are rich with meaning. The result,
however, is not one of second-hand or retouched poetic
painting; for the words are used in new, fresh settings
or they are placed in daring juxtaposition with words not
ordinarily considered poetic, for example:

> At midnight 'neath a maze of stars
> I flame with glittering rime,
> And stand, above the stubble, stiff
> As mail at morning-prime.

This is a quotation from a poem describing a scarecrow;
and in "The Happy Encounter," a line containing the
words *pilgrimage* and *Paradise* is followed by one beginning "He snuffled, grunted, squealed." Furthermore,
whatever debt De la Mare owes to the poets that have
preceded him is paid by words of his own coinage, words
which create their own meaning: "*niminy* fingers" and
"The Fairy *mimbling mambling* in the garden."

Still another of his devices is to use inversions:

> They carried in cages of wicker along,

or

> Three jolly Farmers
> Once bet a pound
> Each dance the others would
> Off the ground.

However much these may be condemned by abstract rules of prosody, in De la Mare's poetry they do not seem lazy substitutes for skill. Never so involved as to obscure meaning, they serve rather to give the effects of surprise and strangeness instrumental in creating tone.

Similar, too, is the handling of rhyme. Delicate, faintly elusive, words do not rhyme in the expected manner; yet because of their very delicacy, their rhyming is satisfying to the ears and to one's inner demands of the poetic. So *wreath* rhyming with *breath,* *stars* with *laughs,* surprise but delight.

Repetition, by which the poet produces almost by hypnotism his desired effect, is used most tellingly in "Silver." The word *silver* runs through the poem, holding together those details which, of themselves, build up the complete picture.

But most characteristic of De la Mare, and most effective, is the music of his meters. His fluent lines are filled with rapid changes in meter, frequent variations from the dominant foot:

> Coral and clear emerald,
> And amber from the sea,
> Lilac-coloured amethyst,
> Chalcedony;
> The lovely Spirit of Air
> Floats on a cloud and doth ride,
> Clad in the beauties of earth
> Like a bride.

As a matter of fact, the old standard of accented and un-accented syllables seems to be abandoned for a time unit. This results in the omission of syllables from conventional feet, as in "The Stranger," or else the use of the unusual four-syllable foot, as in "The Revenant":

O all ye fair ladies with your colours and your graces,
    And your eyes clear in flame of candle and hearth,
Toward the dark of this old window lift not up your smil-
    ing faces,
    Where a Shade stands forlorn from the cold of the
    earth.

Poetry made up entirely of subtle atmosphere, of moon-light and fairies, might easily lay itself open to the charge of tenuousness. But the poetry of De la Mare escapes being merely ephemeral and delicate by two characteris-tics of the poet: a graceful and saving sense of humor, and an interest in people. It is difficult, in some cases, to say, "Here the poet is humorous"; in the larger number of De la Mare's poems one simply senses the brightness of outlook that dispels heavy and untoward seriousness and murkiness. But in *Stuff and Nonsense* the poet has given his sense of the ridiculous full rein. The result is a delightful volume of nonsense, of which "Moonshine," "Green," "Fish," and "Ann's Aunt and the Bear" are simply examples picked at random.

An early indication of the other of the poet's rescuing qualities was given in the poem "The Happy Encounter," wherein Poetry finds the blue of her own eyes reflected in the eyes of Science, the goal of her seeking the same as that of his. A poet who thus realizes the fundamental unity of all thought, must realize, too, the unity of people. So he presents them in his poems, descriptive rather than dramatic, but essentially understanding. And whether the characters are characters from life or characters from books, they are drawn with the same unerring touch of truth. The ten characters from Shakespeare are no less true than are Old Susan, Old Ben, or Miss Loo who, one feels, must have been actual acquaintances.

MERCUTIO

Along an avenue of almond-trees
Came three girls chattering of their sweethearts three.
And lo! Mercutio, with Byronic ease,
Out of his philosophic eye cast all
A mere flowered twig of thought, whereat—
Three hearts fell still as when an air dies out
And Venus falters lonely o'er the sea.
But when within the further mist of bloom
His step and form were hid, the smooth child Ann
Said, "La, and what eyes he had!" and Lucy said,
"How sad a gentleman!" and Katherine,
"I wonder, now, what mischief he was at."
And these three also April hid away,
Leaving the Spring faint with Mercutio.

A somewhat deeper and a more tragic note is struck in "In the Dark," "The Suicide," and "Drugged." De la Mare is touched with humanity and so, in spite of fancy and romance, is a modern. His particular aspect of modernity, however, consists not so much in finding a complete system that embraces and explains all things as in insisting upon the essential importance of each one's identity. His answer to doubt and perplexity he gives in "Even in the Grave": "Even in the grave thou wilt have thyself." He gives it again in "The Imagination's Pride":

. . . O, whithersoever thy vaunting rove,
His deepest wisdom harbours in thy side,
In thine own bosom hides His utmost love.

This force of personality, this key to life as it is the key to poetry, exists not only for mature minds but for children. Nowhere, perhaps, is it more delightfully expressed than in "Mrs. Earth":

Mrs. Earth makes silver black,
    Mrs. Earth makes iron red,
But Mrs. Earth can not stain gold,
    Nor ruby red.
Mrs. Earth the slenderest bone
    Whitens in her bosom cold,
But Mrs. Earth can change my dreams
    No more than ruby or gold.
Mrs. Earth and Mr. Sun
    Can tan my skin, and tire my toes,
But all that I'm thinking of, ever shall think,
    Why, neither knows.

POETICAL WORKS

A CHILD'S DAY	*Henry Holt and Co.*
THE LISTENERS	*Henry Holt and Co.*
PEACOCK PIE	*Henry Holt and Co.*
MOTLEY AND OTHER POEMS	*Henry Holt and Co.*
COLLECTED POEMS, 1901-1918	*Henry Holt and Co.*
THE VEIL AND OTHER POEMS	*Henry Holt and Co.*
DOWN-ADOWN-DERRY	*Henry Holt and Co.*
STUFF AND NONSENSE	*Henry Holt and Co.*
SELECTED POEMS	*Henry Holt and Co.*

ALFRED EDWARD HOUSMAN

ALFRED EDWARD HOUSMAN

IN 1922 a most amazing event occurred in the literary world: a poet published a volume of his poems. The poet was A. E. Housman; the book, *Last Poems*. There were several reasons why this event, which in the case of other writers would have been calmly accepted as the expected in the usual course of things, was in Housman's case hailed as a literary wonder of more than nine days' duration.

In the first place, the book appeared twenty-five years after the publication of his first and only other book of poetry, *A Shropshire Lad*. During those twenty-five years, the poet's point of view toward life remained unchanged. The second volume continued so inevitably the strain of the first, a trifle more subdued, perhaps, but still fresh and still singing the same theme, that the two volumes may be considered as one. In the second place, the poet by his choice of title and by a decisive prefatory note announced the end of his songs. Surely a poet who after so long a silence could produce so vibrant a volume, a poet not yet too old for creative work, might hope to write more verse. But the poet's words seem final, his voluntary muting irrevocable:

"I publish these poems, few though they are, because it is not likely that I shall ever be impelled to write much more. I can no longer expect to be revisited by the continuous excitement under which in the early months of 1895 I wrote the greater part of my other book, nor indeed could I well sustain it if it came; and it is best that what I have written should be printed while I am here to see it through the press and control its spelling and punctuation. About a quarter of the matter belongs to the April of the present year, but most of it to dates between 1895 and 1910."

If something has been hinted of the stir created by *Last Poems*, the complete wonder attached to Housman has not yet been suggested. Housman is a poet of barely a hundred published poems. Yet with so small a quantity of verse he has influenced strongly a whole generation of younger poets. There is a compelling insistence of simplicity and sincerity about his poems. His first volume was the expression of a revolt, conscious or unconscious, against Victorian elaboration. In uncomplicated meters, in the language of everyday life, he expressed the elemental themes of love and death. In contrast to a prevailing complacent religious faith in the essential goodness of the universe, he voiced a philosophy of clear-eyed and brave acceptance of evil and death.

The method and subject matter that struck responsive notes with younger men evolving the new poetry were, doubtless, the very elements that made Housman a poet popular with the soldiers of the great war. St. John Adcock, the British writer and editor, found on a visit to the front in France and Belgium that Housman was one of the three poets most in demand at the rest camps. The wonder of this lies in the fact that Housman has never been a poet advertised to the general reading public with display headlines or fanfare of trumpets.

As a matter of fact, and here is a further anomaly, Housman has not even made writing his career. He is a professor of Latin at Cambridge University, where his chief interest is the elucidation of old Latin texts. On this he brings to bear all his erudition, his painstaking scholarship, his impatience of slovenly work, and a most mordant wit. The quoted preface to his second volume suggests his meticulousness toward details. His critical studies give evidence of the relentless way in which he can express his views. "The wolf," he writes of a commentator with whose opinions he disagrees, "to whom in his proper shape you denied admittance, has come back disguised as your mother the goose, and his gosling has opened the door to him." He works long and painstakingly on a critical edition of the Latin *M. Manilii Astronomicon* and then, when pointing out a contradiction in the text, permits himself the comment: "Liars need not have long memories if they address themselves only to fools, who have short ones, and an astrological poet writing his third book may safely forget his second, because an astrological reader will never remember it."

It is the Housman who teaches and edits whom F. L. Lucas describes in his article, "Few, But Roses," in *The Dial* for September 8, 1924. "With what expectation one waited in the Lecture Theatre of the Arts School, amid an audience that seemed unworthily sparse, for the first sight of the poet—and in what perplexity one went away!

Could this quiet, immaculate figure, setting straight, with even-voiced, passionless, unresting minuteness, the jots and tittles of a fifth-rate ancient whose whole epic was not worth one stanza of his own—could this be the same? Only the lines about the mouth with their look of quiet, unutterable distaste, only the calm, relentless, bitter logic, as of destiny itself, with which some sprawling German commentator was broken into little pieces and dropped into the void, seemed in the least recognizable features."

As a matter of fact, it is only this Housman whom the public has been permitted to know. The Housman of the poems has preserved a reticence through which few details of chronology or of personality have escaped.

He was born, even he must admit, on March 26, 1859, in the western midlands near the Severn Hills. He lived in Worcestershire, now a part of the industrial area of Birmingham, and not in Shropshire itself. But Shropshire, the setting of his poems, with its Ludlow Castle, to which he frequently refers and for which an earlier poet wrote his masque of "Comus," lay within his boyhood's vision. He attended the Bromsgrove School.

His early years must have been rich with the experiences of a country boy, the quick apperceptions of some beauty of the countryside, the intimacy with the people about him, and, above all, the deep friendship of comrades:

> About your work in town and farm
> Still you'll keep my head from harm,
> Still you'll help me, hand that gave
> A grasp to friend me to the grave.

It may well be that when the young man left his home for his university studies at Oxford, the break from his early associations and the introduction into a new environment required adjustments that proved difficult; and the difficulties made the period one gladly forgotten. Whatever the reason may be, of the years at St. John's College, where Housman received the degree of M.A. and of which he is an Honorary Fellow, there is no trace in the material of his poems.

In 1882, after receiving his degree, Housman went to London. But London was a "friendless world" to him and his thoughts turned longingly back to Shropshire:

> Yonder, lightening other loads,
> The seasons range the country roads,
> But here in London streets I ken
> No such helpmates, only men;
> And these are not in plight to bear,
> If they would, another's care.

Yet for a number of years he was to make his home and find his work in London. From 1882 until 1892 he was employed in the Civil Service as a higher division clerk in the Patent Office. In 1892 he became Professor of Latin at the University of London, a chair he filled until 1911. It was in the earlier of these two periods that he wrote his poem in honor of Queen Victoria's Jubilee, "1887":

> Oh, God will save her, fear you not:
> Be you the men you've been,
> Get you the sons your fathers got,
> And God will save the Queen.

In the latter period, specifically in 1895, he wrote the larger number of poems appearing in *A Shropshire Lad*, his first volume, published in 1896.

In 1911 the scene of his professorial duties was changed to Cambridge, where he now holds the Latin chair at King's College. There he is immersed in his studies and lectures, contributing an occasional article to some philological magazine; and from there he startled the world—once—with his second volume of poems.

"The literary event of the moment," the London correspondent of the *New York Times* called it when it appeared, and then went on to write, "I have never met Alfred Edward Housman, and I have never met a man who had met him."

Fortunately, however, there is one record of a man who did meet Housman and who appreciated the charm of his personality. In his diary, on Sunday, November 26, 1911, the British diplomat, traveler, and writer, Wilfrid Scawen Blunt, makes the following entry:

"I took Housman for a walk and asked him how he had come to write his early verses and whether there was any episode in his life which suggested their gruesome character, but he assured me it was not so. He had lived as a boy in Worcestershire, not in Shropshire, though within sight of the Shropshire hills, and there was nothing gruesome to record. He shows no trace now of anything romantic, being a typical Cambridge Don, prim in his manner, silent, and rather shy, conventional in dress and manner, learned, accurate, and well informed. He is professor there of Latin, talking fairly well, but not brilliantly or with any originality, depressed in tone, and difficult to rouse to any strong expression of opinion. Nevertheless, I like him, and with Meynell's help we got him to discuss his own poems, though he refused absolutely to read them out. He read instead one of mine, in response to my having read one of his, 'Is My Team Ploughing?' I have a great admiration for his *Shropshire Lad,* on account of its ballad qualities, and the wonderful certainty in his choice of exactly the right word. We had much pleasant talk all day, and sat up again till twelve at night telling ghost stories. He takes an interest in these. Housman's personal appearance is one of depression and indifferent health. He does not smoke, drinks little, and would, I think, be quite silent if he were allowed to be."

This poet, who seems to prefer silence, has, however, in his two volumes of poetry, vocalized the thoughts and feelings of a vast number of people. He has for them expressed beautifully and succinctly in concrete form definite attitudes toward the fundamental problems of life and death.

The poems of his two volumes have then an essential unity, both of material and of mood. They center about country folk, about soldiers, or young people in love or contemplating the future. They are definitely poems of the country, poems of fields and trees and flowers; but they are neither the pastoral poems of a shepherdess Phyllis in blue-ribboned picture hat nor the bitter, starkly realistic poems of careworn drudges toiling in sun-drowned fields. Avoiding the extremes of a blind romanticism and of a one-sided realism, they dramatize Hous-

man's own ideas in the lives of everyday folk who have
first worked and played and loved in a small country
town.

If one could reduce these poems to a single central
theme, it might be something of this nature: Life may be
a thing of beauty and joy. But beauty and joy are brief;
emotions change; death overshadows all. Yet, since death
is inevitable, let it be met with acquiescence and boldness.

There are occasional variations on this theme, the celebration perhaps of some boyhood friendship, an insistence
on enjoying to the full the pleasures of the moment, or
an equally insistent welcoming of death as a happy solution to life's cares. But whatever the variation, the mood
of the poems is constant. Throughout there is an underlying sadness, there is a touch of regret, there is an air
of pessimism that at times becomes cynical. Life is a "long
fool's-errand to the grave"; its weary routine is without
meaning or purpose:

> Ten thousand times I've done my best
> And all's to do again.

There are, Housman recognizes, flashes of beauty in
life:

> Loveliest of trees, the cherry now
> Is hung with bloom along the bough,
> And stands about the woodland ride
> Wearing white for Eastertide.

The fading of these beauties, as fade they must, is the
occasion for regret and sorrow:

With rue my heart is laden
  For golden friends I had,
For many a rose-lipt maiden
  And many a lightfoot lad.

By brooks too broad for leaping
  The lightfoot boys are laid;
The rose-lipt girls are sleeping
  In fields where roses fade.

Just as beauty fades and goes, so the emotions change
and vanish:

Good-night, my lad, for nought's eternal;
  No league of ours, for sure.
To-morrow I shall miss you less,
And ache of heart and heaviness
  Are things that time should cure.

Love itself, however earnestly pledged, is not steadfast;
it, too, yields to time, alters, and disappears. A poignant
expression of this thought is "Is My Team Ploughing?"
A dead man questions his dearest friend about the people
and things he has left upon earth:

"Is my girl happy,
  That I thought hard to leave,
And has she tired of weeping
  As she lies down at eve?"

Ay, she lies down lightly,
  She lies not down to weep:
Your girl is well contented.
  Be still, my lad, and sleep.

"Is my friend hearty,
   Now I am thin and pine,
And has he found to sleep in
   A better bed than mine?"

Yes, lad, I lie easy,
   I lie as lads would choose;
I cheer a dead man's sweetheart,
   Never ask me whose.

Occasionally, though rarely, in the face of such imper-
manence, Housman urges a full enjoyment of the present:

Think no more, lad; laugh, be jolly:
   Why should men make haste to die?

But there is the basic thought that only the unthinking
can find life a bright and joyous affair; a thought more
definitely expressed in the poem, "Terence, This is Stupid
Stuff."

Ale, man, ale's the stuff to drink
For fellows whom it hurts to think: . . .
         .   .   .   .   .
Therefore, since the world has still
Much good, but much less good than ill,
And while the sun and moon endure
Luck's a chance, but trouble's sure,
I'd face it as a wise man would,
And train for ill and not for good.

Whatever the line of reasoning may be, the same con-
clusion is reached. Life is beautiful, but brief; or life is
a burden, to be laid down gladly. In either case, death
comes; and, more often than not, it is a welcome release.

It is, in fact, a thing to be accepted uncomplainingly, even joyfully, as a solution of life's difficulties and as a substitute for greater griefs.

> Smart lad, to slip betimes away
> From fields where glory does not stay.
>
> . . . . .
>
> Now you will not swell the rout
> Of lads that wore their honors out,
> Runners whom renown outran
> And the name died before the man.

There is nothing passive in this attitude; there is no evidence of cowardice. There is no pusillanimous yielding to defeat:

> The troubles of our proud and angry dust
> Are from eternity and shall not fail.
> Bear them we can, and if we can we must.
> Shoulder the sky, my lad, and drink your ale.

There is, rather, an exultation in the ability to look death in the face:

> As I strap on for fighting
> My sword that will not save.

There is no whining, no rebellion; there is calm bravery. And, at times, there is humor:

> Wonder 'tis how little mirth
> Keeps the bones of man from lying
> On the bed of earth.

The line between humor and cynicism is but a faint one. An added word, an inflection, and an originally jesting line is filled with the hopeless disillusionment of a man's experience. "Is My Team Ploughing?" is a cynical poem. There is cynicism in Housman's attitude toward lovers who love undyingly—for a moment. There is cynicism, too, in

> And the youth at morning shine
> Makes the vows he will not keep.

But somehow one does not think of Housman as preëminently a cynical poet, any more than one thinks of him as preëminently a pessimistic one. Just as his calmness and his bravery save him from the latter charge, so do the inclusiveness of his thoughts and feelings, his tenderness, and his sorrow save him from the former. His whole-souled celebration of friendship would, alone, mitigate his cynicism:

> I sought them far and found them,
>   The sure, the straight, the brave,
> The hearts I lost my own to,
>   The souls I could not save.
> They braced their belts about them,
>   They crossed in ships the sea,
> They sought and found six feet of ground,
>   And there they died for me.

In addition to the young people who live in the shadow of Ludlow, who walk country lanes, plow the fields, and play village football, Housman uses for the dramatic center of his poems those who as young recruits leave Shropshire to join the army. He draws no falsely glamorous picture of a soldier's life; the soldier leaves his home to face inevitable death. But the prayers and the hopes of his home people go with him; they manifest their intense pride in him; they are confident of his courage; they know that he will maintain the honor that is Shropshire's.

It is the pride of Shropshire that Housman celebrates, rather than a nationalized patriotism. It is as though all his tender feelings clung so tightly to one small place that they did not have the opportunity to become attached to any other. London is disliked. England as an inclusive motherland is not mentioned. It is always Shropshire for which the heart yearns; it is always Shropshire that sets the standards of conduct:

> You and I must keep from shame
> In London streets the Shropshire name.

This love of Shropshire can flower into a tender lyric like that of " 'Tis Time, I Think, by Wenlock Town," wherein the poet's longing to see the broom and hawthorn in spring blossom once more becomes the universalized nostalgia of mankind:

> Oh tarnish late on Wenlock Edge,
>   Gold that I never see;
> Lie long, high snowdrifts in the hedge
>   That will not shower on me.

The emotional intensity which here finds voice is present in a number of other lyrics. It is never loud nor thunderously passionate; but calm and controlled, gentle and restrained, it has increased force and effectiveness. Such a lyric is "The Halfmoon Westers Low, My Love," or

"Sinner's Rue," or "From Far, From Eve and Morning," or the delicate lyric beginning:

> White in the moon the long road lies,
> The moon stands blank above;
> White in the moon the long road lies
> That leads me from my love.

The outstanding characteristic of these lyrics, as indeed of all Housman's poems, is their supreme simplicity, a simplicity of presentation as well as of idea. The language of these poems is the language of everyday speech; their rhythm, the rhythm of common talk. "Is My Team Ploughing?" and "Loveliest of Trees, the Cherry Now" are excellent examples of this; so, too, is the poem beginning:

> When I was one-and-twenty
> I heard a wise man say,
> "Give crowns and pounds and guineas
> But not your heart away;
> Give pearls away and rubies
> But keep your fancy free."
> But I was one-and-twenty,
> No use to talk to me.

There is in this simple diction, and in the occasional appearance of a folk-word, the true ballad effect, an effect that is heightened by the manner in which the poetical idea is developed. There are present the ballad characteristics of simple uncomplicated incidents, of the suppression of details, of a background hint of something mysterious and still to be explained. "The Carpenter's Son" and "The True Love" show how close to the folk ballad in form and in method many of Housman's poems come.

Yet the apparent simplicity is, after all, somewhat deceptive. Words are freighted with more than their usual significance. They reveal implied depths of meaning; and a few lines are made to yield a highly concentrated tragedy. Consider, for example, "Bredon Hill," which in simplicity, mood, and implication is so typically a Housman poem. Or consider the story implied in this poem of two stanzas:

> When I came last to Ludlow
>   Amidst the moonlight pale,
> Two friends kept step beside me,
>   Two honest lads and hale.
>
> Now Dick lies long in the churchyard,
>   And Ned lies long in jail,
> And I come home to Ludlow
>   Amidst the moonlight pale.

Even more concentrated is the story in the two lines:

> When he will hear the stroke of eight
> And not the stroke of nine.

Because of the absolute rightness of word and rhythm, two further characteristics of Housman's poems are sometimes overlooked. One is the variety of his meters; the other, his felicity of diction. The simple ballad quatrain would, on a hasty glance through the two volumes, seem to be the prevailing verse form. Yet there are actually

a large variety of stanza forms; there are rhyming couplets, and there are five-, six-, seven-, and eight-line
stanzas, in each of which is shown a diversity of rhyme
schemes. Nor are the three-foot and four-foot lines the
only lines used by him. He shows equal dexterity in his
use of longer lines, lines of five feet, as,

The lads in their hundreds to Ludlow come in for the fair;

of six feet, as,

Be still, my soul, be still; the arms you bear are brittle;

and of seven feet, as in "The New Mistress,"

I will go where I am wanted to a lady born and bred
Who will dress me free for nothing in a uniform of red.

Even in the short-lined stanza, however, there is such
flexibility in the unit foot and in the placing of the pause
that an infinite variety of effects is produced. So one comes
upon a sudden pause in a line as in "Wake: the silver dusk
returning"; or variations from the predominating foot in
such stanzas as,

> The soldier's is the trade:
> In any wind or weather
> He steals the heart of maid
> And man together.

and

> The orchards half the way
> From home to Ludlow fair
> Flowered on the first of May
> In Mays when I was there;

And seen from stile or turning
The plume of smoke would show
Where fires were burning
That went out long ago.

So, too, for all the effect of simplicity, there is vivid word-painting. The aspen, Housman says, shakes its "rainy-sounding silver leaves." "The chestnut casts his flambeaux." "The sloe was lost in flower." A steeple clock "sprinkles the quarters."

Or beeches strip in storms for winter
And stain the wind with leaves.

Because of his unerring but unobtrusive craftsmanship, because of the directness of his ideas, it is easy to understand the hold Housman has on his readers. If his poems lack storms of passion, they possess the certainty and sureness of milder moods and feelings. And whether their philosophy is, or is not, the fundamental philosophy of the reader, the poems themselves are so inevitably right!

The poems as a transmutation of Housman's own experiences have still to be explained. This can be done, however, only when Housman himself consents to reveal the clew. One wishes for such a revelation. One wishes, too, for more poems from the poet who feels he has sung his last. The lover of poetry rebels against Housman's farewell which, however moving and beautiful, comes all too soon:

The lofty shade advances,
I fetch my flute and play:

Come, lads, and learn the dances
And praise the tune to-day.
To-morrow, more's the pity,
Away we both must hie,
To air the ditty,
And to earth I.

POETICAL WORKS

A SHROPSHIRE LAD   *Henry Holt and Company*
LAST POEMS   *Henry Holt and Company*

RUDYARD KIPLING

RUDYARD KIPLING

RUDYARD KIPLING

Much I owe to the Lands that grew—
More to the Lives that fed—
But most to Allah Who gave me two
Separate sides to my head.
          —"The Two-sided Man."

THERE is a story that when Rudyard Kipling was a very little boy living in Bombay, he one day set out for a walk with a native farmer. Placing his hand in that of his companion, he turned to his mother and in Hindostani called to her, "Good-by, this is my brother."

Thus early did Kipling identify himself with the vast, rich India about him. Thus did he manifest that brotherliness that was to embrace many types and races of people, that was to claim a certain kinship with the animals, and was to endow even inanimate objects like machinery and ships with some of the qualities of his fellow men and women. If in this attitude there was to be at times a touch of superiority, a suggestion of condescending bigbrotherliness, it is understandable; for in that relationship between two races of which the little boy was first aware, the relationship between the English and the native

Indian, there was never the element of complete equality and democracy.

However, it was as brother that the boy thought and spoke of his brown companion. That was one aspect of the "two-sided man." The other aspect was his own inescapable Englishness, the tradition of English service and culture that he had inherited from both his father and his mother. His father, John Lockwood Kipling, the eldest son of a clergyman, was an artist. One day at a picnic at a lake between the little towns of Rudyard and Bushton, he met Alice Macdonald, the daughter of a Wesleyan minister. He fell in love with her and married her. Her family, too, was an interesting one, one in which talented women had married men of talent. One sister, Georgiana, married Edmund Burne-Jones, the painter. Another sister, Agnes, married Edward Poynter, who was to become president of the Royal Academy. A third sister, Louise, married Alfred Baldwin, the iron-master; their son, Stanley Baldwin, the British statesman, is thus the poet's cousin. As for Alice Kipling, the poet's mother, she was noted for her beauty and charm, her wit, and her ability to write verse and to tell a story.

Life for the young Mr. and Mrs. Kipling, centering in the Kensington Art Schools of London and in their artistic friends, seemed calmly established and very far removed from events on the other side of the globe. But about this time, the early 1860's, Bombay in India was becoming an important commercial center. The city was growing tremendously, and the English government felt that it should have some artistic supervision. So Mr.

Kipling was appointed professor of Architectural Sculpture in the British School of Art and he and Mrs. Kipling left England to make their home in Bombay.

There on December 30, 1865, their son was born. He was named Joseph Rudyard. According to a tale, since denied by the poet, the name Rudyard was suggested by the baby's aunt, Lady Burne-Jones, to commemorate the lake where the romance of his parents had begun. Though not true, it is a pleasing story and one that would account for the odd and individual name—the Joseph having been dropped—by which the poet is known.

Life in India must have been very thrilling and full for the little boy. There were all manner of things to be seen, all manner of tales to be heard. English people of culture gathered at his parents' home and enunciated English thoughts and principles. Indian traditions and ideals were taught him by his Indian friends and very particularly by his native nurses. He learned to speak fluently a number of Indian dialects. He knew India and its ways. And so he became the heir of two old and rich civilizations.

Life in India, however, was not an ideal one for English children. In England a healthier childhood could be assured and an infinitely better education. So English children—children of four or five—were sent away from their parents in India to English schools and homes that their parents had known in their own youth.

Thus it happened that in 1871 Rudyard and his younger sister went to live at Southsea near Portsmouth with the wife of a retired naval officer. Though there had been

an earlier visit to England in 1868, it must have been
the memory of this later ocean voyage that is recalled in
the lines in "How the Whale Got His Throat":

> When the cabin port-holes are dark and green
>   Because of the seas outside;
> When the ship goes *wop* (with a wiggle between)
> And the steward falls into the soup-tureen,
>   And the trunks begin to slide;
> When Nursey lies on the floor in a heap,
> And Mummy tells you to let her sleep,
> And you aren't waked or washed or dressed,
> Why, then you will know (if you haven't guessed)
> You're "Fifty North and Forty West!"

Little is known of the Southsea stay except that the
children's natural loneliness was somewhat mitigated by
the nearness of their aunt, Lady Burne-Jones; and that
the woman in whose care they were entrusted was much
given to Bible reading. Biblical phraseology, possibly
harking back to this period of Kipling's life, is echoed
in his poetry, in his casual allusions to "morning stars"
and to cherubim and seraphim, and in his lines:

Down the desert, down the railway, down the river,
    Like Israelites from bondage so he came,
'Tween the clouds o' dust and fire to the land of his desire,
    And his Moses, it was Sergeant Whatisname!

In 1878 the boy accompanied his father to Paris, where
he visited the Art Exhibit. Under his father's instruction
and devotion—and there was always to be a devoted in-

timacy between father and son—Kipling was shown the beauties and treasures of the French capital. But the delightful interlude was a brief one; later in the year, the boy was enrolled for his schooling in the United Services College, at Westward Ho! near Bideford, Devon.

The school, later to be immortalized in the schoolboy saga of *Stalky and Co.*, wherein Beetle is the fictionalized picture of young Kipling, was not one of England's old, recognized "public" schools. It had been established as recently as 1864, near the Westward Ho! golf course, in a group of buildings that had formed part of an unsuccessful land-development scheme.

The school had one or two hundred pupils of most of whom an army career was expected; in fact, the school's chief purpose was to prepare its pupils for Sandhurst, the English military academy. In this purpose Kipling did not share. Nor does he seem to have participated to any great extent in the general activities of his schoolmates; he was an excellent swimmer, but swimming apparently was the only sport in which he showed any real interest.

He did become, however, an editor of the school paper, the *United Services College Chronicle*; and the duties of his position serving as justification, he was not only excused from some of the school's usually required athletics, but was given the free privilege of the library of the headmaster, Mr. Cornwall Price, a friend of Kipling Senior. Mr. G. C. Beresford, one of Kipling's schoolmates, the original of McTurk in *Stalky and Co.*, writes in the *New York Times* for December 23, 1928, concerning Kipling's reading:

"Kipling was one on whom such privileges were by no means wasted. He was such an omnivorous reader that two libraries were by no means too large a feast. He read at an enormous speed, holding the book close to his eyes, with his four fingers inserted into the leaves, ready to turn over a leaf every three seconds. His eyes skimmed down the pages as if the printing were down the page and not across; five or six lines were read at a time, and yet the meaning of the text was perfectly absorbed, as we frequently proved by snatching the book from his hands and questioning him as to the precise contents of the last six pages."

His editorial duties, which his reading was to serve, lasted from Number IV of the *Chronicle*, that of June 30, 1881, through Number X, July 24, 1882. Number IV contained his journalistic creed: "It is our intention to make the *Chronicle* as readable and concise an epitome of these [the school's activities] as we can, looking to each boy in the school to help us." Most of the writing was done by Kipling himself. His literary ability, evidently, was early recognized. Again Mr. Beresford is quoted: "I had never seen boys with his capacity for literary expression; they may have had certain power of writing lame descriptions, of making halting verses in a hesitating manner and with single syllable and obvious rhymes; but here was sizzling, fizzling literary impulse —with a small boy tacked on behind."

The *Chronicle* alone was not sufficient to contain his work. He wrote for the *Bideford Journal*. Some of his verses were published in a London paper. Others appeared in *The Scribbler*. *The Scribbler* was a magazine written on foolscap paper and issued through 1879 and 1880 by the Burne-Jones cousins—with whom, at the Grange in South Kensington, Kipling spent his vacations —and by the children of William Morris. In it Kipling's writing appears under the nom de plume of Nickson. In 1881 *Schoolboy Lyrics* appeared, a collection of twenty-three of his poems brought together by his parents.

While at school, he was a member of a Literary Society that held debates. Once, at least, he took part in a school play, acting Sir Anthony Absolute in a performance of *The Rivals*, December 20, 1881. And he won one prize in literature. In spite of this, however, his general scholarship was not so high as to make him an outstanding pupil; and he was not conspicuously popular with his fellow students. His reading and writing must have absorbed most of his schoolboy energies.

In 1883, however, school days ended. The years at school, though comparatively few, were not without effect upon the boy. If classroom lessons were a matter of more or less indifference, still, education was got in the wide reading that the boy did. His literary interests were stimulated and the work for the *Chronicle* directed these interests to their natural channel. Furthermore, the school itself, with its standards and newly established traditions, shaped his general outlook upon life. It insisted upon the military ideas of organization and obedience; its student body exacted adherence by bullying and baiting recalcitrant boys. "A School Song" praises the school masters who, beating with rods "for the love they bore us," taught the lessons of common sense, loyalty to a task, and obedience to orders.

These ideals, carried over into national life, were expressed in a poem, "Ave Imperatrix," which appeared in *The Chronicle* of March 1882. The poem, written to celebrate Queen Victoria's escape from an attack on her life, contains the significant stanza:

> And all are bred to do your will
> By land and sea—wherever flies
> The flag, to fight and follow still
> And work your Empire's destinies.

This attitude of the consecration of the individual to the group's task, particularly to the task of working out England's destiny in forming a vast empire, was to characterize much of Kipling's verse.

When he left school, Kipling was permitted to choose between further study at a university and a return to India. He chose the latter and thus made what must be considered a momentous decision. For when he arrived in India, going to Lahore where his family then lived, a city two and a half days from Bombay, he was given on the strength of his school editing a position on *The Civil and Military Gazette*. He was now definitely embarked on the career of a journalist. The journalistic mind, even after he severed newspaper connections, colored his work. It prompted him to recognize appealing things of the moment and make them important; to seize current popular attitudes and express them, rather than to reveal his own self.

As sub-editor of the *Gazette*, his duties consisted of assembling telegrams from all parts of the British Empire, of organizing material from other newspapers, and of working government reports into readable articles. He appeared at work in the morning dressed for the Indian heat in white cotton trousers and a thin vest. By the end of the day, his costume was polka-dotted from his careless habit of nervously shaking an inky pen. Thus decorated, he must have presented an amazing appearance —short, stooped, sallow-complexioned, with heavy eyebrows over eyes peering through thick spectacles. But whatever his appearance, he showed at his work a deftness and industry that won from his superior the commendation, "He was a staff in himself."

From the time that he became a member of the *Gazette* staff he was an indefatigable writer of prose and verse. The inspiration for the latter frequently came from the concerts that the native police bands gave in the public gardens; for a poem would suggest itself first as a definite rhythm from something which he heard played.

These early poems appeared frequently as column fillers in *The Gazette*. In that function they won the high critical praise of the native press foreman, Rukh-Din. "Your poetry, very good, sir," he would say; "just coming proper length today."

The poems were often satiric pictures of life in India, of native officials, of the English sent out to govern, of the social existence of men and women living in Simla to escape the heat. After a short time, these verses were collected from the newspapers in which they had appeared and were printed in a book made to resemble a government report. *Departmental Ditties*, the book was called, and it was sold by postcard by the author himself. The profits, Kipling said, went directly from publisher to author, being transferred from one of his pockets to another. The edition was soon exhausted. Other editions followed. "But," writes Kipling in an article, "My First Book," in *McClure's Magazine* for November 1894, "I loved it best when it was a little brown baby with a pink string around its stomach; a child's child, ignorant that it was afflicted with all the most modern ailments; and before people had learned, beyond doubt, how its author lay awake of nights in India, plotting and scheming to write something that should 'take' with the English public."

After five years on the *Gazette*, Kipling was transferred in 1887 to *The Allahabad Pioneer*, the most influential of the Indian journals. He visited various soldiers' camps throughout India; deepened his knowledge of the country; and wrote vivid sketches and tales of native and of Anglo-Indian life that were published in 1888 in Calcutta as *Tales from the Hills*. A number of his stories were printed in small, cheap editions as parts of the Wheeler Indian Railway Library, to be sold on railroad newsstands. Kipling was by now a literary celebrity —in India!

In 1889 he began a tour around the world for the *Pioneer*. The travel articles he wrote appeared serially in that paper and then were brought out as a book, *From Sea to Sea*. He journeyed eastward, arriving in San Francisco on his way home to England. His letters from America stirred up storms of protest. It is true that he was impressed by the American girls. "They are clever," he wrote, "they can talk. Yea, it is said that they think.—They can take care of themselves; they are superbly independent." But for the greater part, his opinions of America were not flattering and his caustic comments called forth the anger that he himself expected when he wrote, "Protect me from the wrath of an outraged community if these letters be ever read by American eyes."

Some of his criticism was deserved. But if any of it was unfair or exaggerated, if the total effect was one of disapprobation rather than of approval or of unbiased presentation, there were several obvious reasons. In the first place, writing must inevitably be colored by its purpose; and the purpose of his letters was to amuse distant readers. In such a situation an interesting, if slightly exaggerated, fact is more satisfactory material than complete truth. Then, too, Kipling had a disdain for democracy that made it difficult for him to understand the American outlook. Moreover, he had a just cause for complaint against certain American publishers. Because of the lack of international copyright laws, a number of his stories had been published in this country without permission from him and with no compensation for him. Though such stories had appeared, their author was not sufficiently well known to be welcomed as a celebrity. He was treated simply as another British traveler and not as the literary genius who was soon to be world-famous.

Kipling's efforts to make connections in America for

his work were unsuccessful. In San Francisco, he was given a trial assignment for *The Examiner;* but his work failed to satisfy and he was not engaged. In New York, he was unable to find a publisher who would accept his stories. His chagrin must have been great; but it could never have equaled the chagrin of those same publishers when, in a few years, popular demand for Kipling's work showed them how lacking in judgment they had been.

By no means daunted in spirit, Kipling reached England. As a matter of fact, his travels had given him a new vision for his work, the desire to sing the song of the English, to express the soul of English-speaking races wherever their lands might be. Fired with this ambition, he definitely set out on his career of independent writing. He took up his residence on an upper floor in a gloomy building in the Strand in London. His room showed evidences of his travels and his interests. "Persian rugs, Japanese screens, a pipe-rack, a magazine rifle, scrapbooks, a great variety of rods and fishing tackle, a box of black Indian cheroots, and a huge jar of smoking tobacco, pictures of military subjects by some of the cleverest French painters, a map of Afghanistan, sketches in black and white by his father—these are the principal objects which catch the eye of a visitor to Kipling's chambers." [1]

There he worked assiduously at his writing. And there for a time he had to struggle against disappointment because his ability was not immediately recognized. That period of struggle and unsuccessful effort was brief. *Plain*

[1] *Bookbuyer,* October 1890.

Tales was republished. It sold but slowly, it is true. But with the republication of *Departmental Ditties*, the *London Academy* critic hailed him. "This book gives promise," he wrote, "of a new literary star rising in the East." By 1890 his popular reputation was established. An American magazine of book news speaks of him as the man whose name a year before had been unknown but for whose work every one was then eager. Kipling clubs were formed. Editors now came to him asking him for his work. After another voyage in 1891, one that took him to still more divisions of the British Empire, to Africa, Australia, Ceylon, and New Zealand, he published *Barrack Room Ballads.*

With the publication of this book, there was a division in the camp of Kipling readers. Critics called the verses doggerel and music-hall rhymes; they objected to their slang and their coarseness; Kipling was said to be speaking with "the voice of the Hooligan." Others, recognizing some of the deficiencies, some of the lapses from the current standards of good taste, still welcomed the freshness and force of the poems. As for the general reading public, they welcomed his writing with delight and clamored for more and more Kipling.

What was the reason for this popularity? A new writer can make an immediate appeal if his subject matter is new and his style original. Kipling opened up a new world for his readers. With intimate knowledge of their beauty and their complexity he presented the continents of Asia and of Africa to an English people becoming conscious of their own destiny as empire-builders. And he presented them in a style that was intimate and individual, bound not at all by any dictates of his predecessors.

The time, moreover, was opportune for just that sort of material and just that kind of free, energetic writing. The public was growing tired, on the one hand, of the prudishness of the Victorian era; and, on the other, of the over-wrought delicacy and decadence of the pre-Raphaelite movement.' Kipling came with a marching swing and outpaced the mincing steps of his contemporaries; he sang boldly and freely of life, of activity, of joy in the present. And people approved. Everybody —that indefinite, but important everybody, that withholds or bestows popular approval—knew "Danny Deever," "Fuzzy-Wuzzy," "Tommy," "Gunga Din," and "Mandalay."

In 1892, the popular writer married Caroline Balestier, an American, and the sister of Wolcott Balestier, with whom Kipling had collaborated in writing a book. Her family was a Vermont family and so to Brattleboro, Vermont, Kipling and his bride went to make their home. They lived in a house on the Balestier land until their own house was completed. This they called Naulahka, which literally means "Costing nine lahks" and figuratively means very dear or precious. There two children were born. And there Kipling wrote a number of volumes, the *Jungle Books, Captains Courageous, Seven Seas,* and *Many Inventions.*

The intimacy of the Kipling home life was jealously guarded. Details were not given to form the material for literary gossip. This retirement and this personal reticence have been generally maintained through the years, to be broken only by the announcement of some significant piece of news.

Kipling lived in Vermont for five years. Thereafter his life was punctuated by his travels and by his books —books of short stories, novels, volumes of poetry. In 1897, after a journey to South Africa, Kipling returned to England and established his home in Rottingdean, Sussex, four miles from Brighton. In February 1899 he came to this country again for a visit. His boat, the ice-coated *Majestic*, was met by a pilot who, recognizing Kipling on board, began to quote some of Kipling's verse. The poet was delighted; but his delight did not make him expansive in an interview which the newspaper ship-reporters sought. Kipling had nothing to say beyond this statement of an artist's creed: "Every effort of art is an effort to be sincere. There is no surer guide, I am sure, than the determination to tell the truth that one feels."

It was, then, the force of his writing, rather than that of his personality, that had a hold on the public. How great this hold was was evidenced the following winter when Kipling lay sick with pneumonia in a New York hotel. Bulletins on his condition were issued frequently; late at night reporters crowded about the board for the latest news; newspapers carried reports; his illness was a matter of common talk and of general concern. Street-car conductors inquired for the latest tidings; celebrities all over the world sent sympathetic messages. A despatch arrived from the German emperor for Mrs. Kipling: "God grant that he may be spared to you and to all that are thankful to him for the soul-stirring way in which he has sung about the deeds of our great common race."

Kipling's daughter, stricken also with pneumonia, died; but Kipling on Easter Day was well enough to write a note of thanks for the solicitude shown by the American people. In their sympathy with Kipling in his sorrow, and in their rejoicing at his recovery, England and America were drawn closer to each other, a fact which prompted from Mark Twain in a speech that spring at the Authors' Club in London one of his dearly loved witticisms: "Since England and America have been joined in Kipling, may they not be severed in Twain."

On his return once more to England, Kipling made his home in the calm, sleepy town of Burwash, Sussex, where he still lives. His house, a gray Elizabethan farmhouse, with "1634" carved over one low door, nestles among the hills, its six tall chimneys visible from a distance. It is called Bateman's. The name is said to be an abbreviation of Abateman's, the origin of which lies in the fact that the forge-master supposed to have built the house had the reputation of "abating" the wages of his men.

At Bateman's, Kipling lives the life of an English country gentleman. He raises Jersey cattle. He goes fishing. Dressed in rough tweeds, he tramps the countryside, undisturbed by his neighbors. It is a retired life, to which few visitors from the outside world gain admittance.

But once a person is admitted and once Kipling's reserve is broken, the visitor finds a charming host, alert, sensitive, with a genial sense of humor. Arthur B. Maurice

in "A Visit to Rudyard Kipling," in *The Mentor* for
February 1928, describes the poet's spirit and fire:

"But here was no old man. Here was youth, surprising,
startling. Youth, an almost boyish youth, was in every
movement of the rather slight figure clad in Norfolk
jacket and knickerbockers, in the springy step, in every
quick, nervous gesture, in the intonation of voice, in the
animation of every utterance. About him was the aura of
a youth unquenchable."

In Sussex, Kipling, the world traveler, is spiritually at
rest. He has made a rediscovery of England; after explor-
ing Asia and Africa, he has come to know the land of his
ancestors. He is able in a short time and in a short space
to traverse the centuries of English history and tradition.
His sentiments cling closely to the England of *Puck of
Pook's Hill* and of *Rewards and Fairies*. There has been
an intensification of the English side of the two-sided
young man, a personal experiencing of what in most of
his youth and young manhood was simply a matter of inheritance and report.

There have been occasional interruptions to the Burwash retirement, events that have brought Kipling into
public print. In 1907 he was awarded the Nobel Prize
for literature, the first Englishman to win the award and
one of the youngest ever to win it; it was given "in con-
sideration of the power of observation, originality of imagination, and also the manly strength in the art of perception and delineation that characterize the writings of
this world-renowned author." In the same year he received
an honorary degree from Oxford.

In 1922 he was made a rector of St. Andrews University in Scotland; and in 1923, when he was made Lord Rector, he delivered a thoughtful speech on "Independence." The same interest was attracted by this speech as years before had been attracted by his talk to the students of McGill University, wherein he had denounced the desire for mere money as a motivating impulse of a person's life.

But it was in connection with the World War that Kipling sacrificed his preferred privacy. In that war he lost his son John, a boy barely eighteen, a member of the Irish Guards; and nothing could prevent a sympathizing public from sharing in his grief. In addition, Kipling himself sought publicity. The war called forth all his early feelings, his intense belief in his country, his more intense hatred of any enemy that might threaten England, and his conviction that any task must be thoroughly and conclusively completed. So he issued statements and wrote poems about the war; he denounced the enemy; he urged their unqualified defeat.

When Kipling writes poetry of any political significance he is likely to arouse antagonistic points of view. As a matter of fact, he has always shown an ability to stir up controversy. Much bitterness was provoked by "The Truce of the Bear," which cautioned England against Russia; by "The Rowers," which condemned Germany, on its first writing because of Germany's attitude toward Venezuela's debt, on its republication because of her part in the World War; by "Our Lady of the Snows," which spoke of Canada's cold; and by "The Rhyme of the Three Captains," which criticized American publishers.

But in any argument, Kipling has always shown bravery and daring. Particularly in his political and governmental views, he has taken a firm and unshakable stand; and always that stand has been for a highly organized, heavily armed British Empire.

"I have," he once said in a speech delivered at the Canadian Club of Winnipeg in October 1907, "I confess it now, done my best for about twenty years to make all the men of the sister nations within the Empire interested in each other."

The loftiest expression of his belief in England as the builder of an empire is, doubtless, "Recessional," which he wrote for the Queen's Jubilee.

> The tumult and the shouting dies;
>   The Captains and the Kings depart:
> Still stands Thine ancient sacrifice,
>   An humble and a contrite heart.
> Lord God of Hosts, be with us yet,
> Lest we forget—lest we forget!

In other poems he expresses all shades of opinion leading up to and down from the exalted mood of "Recessional." There is the ever-present sense of patriotism, a patriotism which in Kipling is closely linked to pride of conquest and which is much more vocal than it is in the usual Englishman. In "A Song of the English" he declares that the Lord must be served, for "He hath smote for us a pathway to the ends of all the Earth!" Hold to the Faith and keep to the Law, he admonishes; and then in "The White Man's Burden," he urges the task of bringing help, though unwanted, to the lesser races, the task of conquest and organization in spite of difficulties and discouragement:

> Take up the White Man's burden—
> Have done with childish days—
> The lightly proffered laurel,
> The easy, ungrudged praise.
> Comes now, to search your manhood
> Through all the thankless years,
> Cold, edged with dear-bought wisdom,
> The judgment of your peers!

This is an expression of the aristocratic theory of *noblesse oblige*; it is the attitude of a superior, conscious of his superiority. One seeks vainly for evidence in Kipling of a belief in democracy. In "A Servant When He Reigneth" and in "MacDonough's Song" there is positive criticism hurled against the theory that the people are the ultimate and proper source of government and of law.

A political doctrine such as this finds its strength in armed force. First, there must be strength of number and of organization, and so Kipling insists upon a closely knit empire to stand against enemies of Britain's benevolent progress. And there must be strength of arms to defend that progress and, when necessary, to fight for it. He is impatient at costly errors like those that were made in the Boer War, at inadequate preparations, and at half-heart-

edly militant campaigns. Such impatience he expresses in
"The Lesson," in "The Old Men," and in "The
Islanders."

Ancient, effortless, ordered, cycle on cycle set,
Life so long untroubled, that ye who inherit forget
It was not made with the mountains, it is not one with the
    deep.
Men, not gods, devised it. Men, not gods, must keep.
Men, not children, servants, or kinsfolk called from afar,
But each man born in the Island broke to the matter of
    war.

The logical outcome of such war-mindedness is some
such upheaval as the World War. The war inspired
Kipling to write poetry that still did not reject his mili-
taristic point of view but did express the bewilderment,
the sense of loss, shared by so many people. "The Children," mourning the loss of young soldiers, defiantly demands expiation. In "My Boy Jack," however, there is the
universalized expression of personal loss:

"Have you news of my boy Jack?"
    Not this tide.
"When d'you think that he'll come back?"
    Not with this wind blowing, and this tide.

And in "For All We Have and Are" is a statement of the
ideals for which such sacrifices were made:

What stands if Freedom fall?
Who dies if England live?

It is because of such definite convictions as Kipling has expressed in his verse, that he has been so provocative a storm-center. It is these beliefs that turn readers of his poems into partisans; that divide them into ardent followers or equally ardent critics. In the ensuing noise and confusion, much of his verse is overlooked, verse that may be considered as poetry and not as political arguments. What of Kipling the poet?

As a poet, he widened the boundaries of poetry so that it might include much that previously had been denied it. He has found poetry in new and unexpected places. Just as in "The King," "Romance brought up the nine-fifteen," so Kipling has brought back the old gods of poetry or provided new gods that are no less satisfying. He himself has been the answer to the prayers of M'Andrew, "Lord, send a man like Robbie Burns to sing the Song O' Steam!" And so he has written his poetry about the wonders of machinery and industry, of engines, and boats, and trains.

For him these are the instruments by which man's work is carried on; and it is in the work of the world that Kipling is interested. Ceaseless activity is the burden of his song; active accomplishment, his insistence. So the runner undeterred by dangers of weather or of country is praised in "Overland Mail"; and in "The Liner She's a Lady," it is the busy "little cargo-boats" who are the true heroes of the poem. Grateful acknowledgment is made in "The Sons of Martha" to those who toil for the comfort and safety of others. The effect upon the workers themselves, their satisfaction at completing a task, their glory in accomplishment, is nowhere better expressed than in "The Explorer," the poem of the man who heeded the call to go on and on, who opened up the unknown country:

Anybody might have found it—but—His whisper came to Me!

Or again in "The Galley-Slave," wherein the rower, released from his grueling toil, recalls the hardships he has endured, then adds:

But to-day I leave the galley. Shall I curse her service then?
God be thanked! Whate'er comes after, I have lived and toiled with Men!

So, too, Kipling's poems of the sea are chiefly poems of work, wherein boats and the ocean provide the setting. He does, it is true, give brief vivid sketches of the sea, as in "The Wet Litany," and in "Anchor Song"; but in "The Sea and the Hills," the poem in which the beauties of the sea are, possibly, most definitely and satisfactorily described, they are presented merely as standards of comparison by which to judge the hillmen's love for their Hill!

Much more than for his songs of work, however, is Kipling important for his songs of the British soldier. He is truly the creator of Tommy Atkins, at all events of the Tommy Atkins of popular conception. It is a further evidence of the liberalization of his poetry that it is the private about whom he writes, not the officer; and it is the common soldier not in his heroic moments, but in his ordinary blustering, roistering life.

I have made for you a song,
And it may be right or wrong,
But only you can tell me if it's true;
I have tried for to explain
Both your pleasure and your pain,
And, Thomas, here's my best respects to you!

So he does not hesitate to show Tommy Atkins when he is drunk, or when he is looting, or even—in the vivid, moving poem "That Day"—when he is running away. He knows the hold that army life has upon its followers; and in "Back to the Army Again" tells the satisfaction of a reënlisted soldier and in "Chant-Pagan" the longing the disbanded soldier has to return to the scenes of his campaigns. He knows the discipline of the army and in "Danny Deever" etches indelibly the effect on a regiment of the execution of one of the men. And he knows the hardships of the soldier, the tedium of the long march that he translates in "Boots"; the sickness that attacks men, that he writes of in "Cholera Camp" and in "The Spies' March"; the small pay and smaller pension that he decries in "Shillin' a Day." Sympathy and understanding color his poems about the soldiers; and for those qualities from the public he pleads in "Tommy":

You talk o' better food for us, an' schools, an' fires, an' all;
We'll wait for extry rations if you treat us rational.
Don't mess about the cook-room slops, but prove it to our
    face
The Widow's Uniform is not the soldier-man's disgrace.

For it's Tommy this, an' Tommy that, an' "Chuck him
    out, the brute!"
But it's "Saviour of 'is country" when the guns begin to
    shoot;
An' it's Tommy this, an' Tommy that, an' any thing you
    please;
An' Tommy ain't a bloomin' fool—you bet that Tommy
    sees!

The soldier who emerges from Kipling's army poems is
an abstraction, a type Tommy Atkins. There are, however,
one or two definitely presented, individualized characters
in Kipling's verse, particularly M'Andrew of "M'Andrew's Hymn" and Sir Anthony Gloster of "The Mary
Gloster." M'Andrew is the Scotch engineer whose soul is
made up of his love of engines and his theological beliefs.
Sir Anthony is the master of a fleet of boats. He has seen
ships change from wood to steel; he has been unscrupulous
in his business actions; he has grown rich. Now, dying, he
asks his only son, a weakling whom he despises, to take
his body on his boat the *Mary Gloster* and to bury him at
sea, where years before his wife had been buried. As for
the boat, itself, as a final gesture that is to be sunk:

Thank Gawd, I can pay for my fancies! Now what's five
    thousand to me,
For a berth off the Paternosters in the haven where I
    would be?

In the two-hundred-odd lines of this poem, the character and career of Sir Anthony become vivid realities. His

story, if only suggested, is plain. Kipling is preëminently a teller of tales and an adept in narrating a ballad. The emphatic quality of verse he recognizes by using short poems to introduce or conclude his prose tales; but, in addition, the narrative skill so marked in his prose is employed in his poetry. No one who has heard of Kipling does not know the story of Gunga Din, the native water carrier who lost his life in giving water to a soldier. No less stirring, and with the added attraction of folk-tale mystery, are the "Ballad of Minepit Shaw" and "The Last Rhyme of True Thomas." "Eddi's Service" is the tenderly told story of the simple priest Eddi, who celebrated Christmas midnight mass. As a contrast to this is "The Ballad of East and West," the story of the Colonel's son, who seeks to capture and punish Kamal, the native chieftain, for having stolen his father's horse. The two men meet. Each recognizes the other's bravery and daring; and in that recognition they swear brotherhood instead of enmity:

But there is neither East nor West, Border, nor Breed nor
    Birth,
When two strong men stand face to face, though they
    come from the ends of the earth!

These stories are told with a detachment and an impersonality that make them seem almost folk ballads, that suggest that Kipling is not interested in poetry as a means of self-revelation and self-expression. There are, however, other poems that to a high degree possess a lyric quality, that reveal the deep emotions of the poet himself. There are, for example, poems about England that in warmth and tenderness are completely different from the intellectualized political poems. "The Flowers" is a delicate poem which symbolizes the love of the English for their land. "Sussex" is an equally tender tribute to the corner of England in which Kipling makes his home.

The more intimate feelings, the emotions arising between people, are not ignored by the poet. There is, for example, the "Love Song of Har Dyal"; and there is the gentle lullaby in the story of "The White Seal"; and the exaltation of mother love in "Mother O' Mine." The clear lyric call of all emotion and of all romance rings out in "The Gipsy Trail":

> The heart of a man to the heart of a maid—
>   Light of my tents, be fleet.
> Morning waits at the end of the world,
>   And the world is all at our feet!

These emotions, which Kipling sings, are fundamental human emotions, universal emotions shared by all mankind. This sense of community has in the poet another aspect, that of continuity of feelings and thoughts through time. "We are very slightly changed," he says, "from the semi-apes who ranged" primitive earth. And so he traces through history the development of a single idea or principle; with his strong historical sense, he delights in showing that the past had the same problems as the present, that the past began work which the present has not yet completed but must, in its turn, hand to the future. This is the underlying mood of such poems as "Natural Theology," "The River's Tale," and "The Palace."

This is the method, too, in "The Land," which in a humorous fashion traces the relationship between land-owner and the true countryman, who possesses—or assumes—more privileges than the owner himself. In Hobden is symbolized all those who through knowledge and use have made the land truly theirs though others possess the legal title and pay the taxes. Hobden, then, illustrates one of Kipling's devices, that of rendering abstract ideas in concrete images. Such a device adds definiteness to his poetry and is one reason for the appeal that his poetry possesses.

This appeal is strengthened by other devices of technique. For one thing the rhythm of his verse is definite, is insistent, as in "Boots," or "The Song of the Banjo"; and is, most usually, in regularly recurring march-time. For another, the verse is catchy; it is filled with clever, memorable phrases: "You're a better man than I am," "soldier and sailor, too," "sisters under the skin." And its effect is emphasized by the use of repetition, sometimes of a single phrase or line, sometimes of a built-up stanza, as in "The Question."

Another device, and a characteristic one, is the use of interpolations, of stage directions, almost. In "Loot," for example, there are such lines, as "(*Cornet:* Toot! toot!)" and

(*ff*) Whoopee! Tear 'im, puppy! Loo! loo! Lulu! Loot! loot! loot!

And in "The Song of the Banjo" the actual sounds of the instrument are introduced, the "tumpa-tumpa-tump" and the "tinka-tinka-tink."

One final element of popularity should be considered. That is the geniality underlying most of the verse. True, at times Kipling manifests a bitterness of spirit and at times an acid satire; but more generally he reveals a sympathy for human behavior, a recognition of the incongruity of things, a sense of the ludicrous, that result in an understanding humor. This humor may reveal itself in a tender smile or else in a hearty laugh, as in "Poseidon's Law," which explains the sailor's well-known propensity for spinning yarns.

The appeal of Kipling's verse, if a popular one, is nevertheless one not primarily emotional. The imagination of the reader is rarely stimulated. The imagination, after all, is subjective, personal, individual. Kipling's poems are, for the most part, not subjective in mood or in purpose; they result from Kipling's social sense and they are directed to the social sense of the reader. This is the natural result of Kipling's philosophy. The Law of the Jungle is more important than the individual; the keystone of the law is "Obey!"

> The game is more than the player of the game,
> And the ship is more than the crew!

There is the necessity for individual development, for individual fitness, as Kipling insists in the "Preface" to *Land and Sea Tales* and in "If"; the individual is important, however, not for himself, but for the whole.

That is the essence of Kipling's belief as he observes

life. It is, moreover, his purpose to observe life critically, to face its realities and to "draw the Thing as he sees It for the God of Things as They Are." If the commonplace as Kipling presents it has some of the glamor of romance, if the real seems at times not entirely clear, then it must be that Kipling occasionally slips away from the calm, steady England of his Sussex, heeding the call of the East, the call of "Mandalay": "Come you back, you British soldiers; come you back to Mandalay!"

For, after all, Kipling remains two-sided. He is a Westerner and an Easterner, a realist and a romanticist, a modern and a reactionary, an unhonored politician and a beloved poet!

POETICAL WORKS

DEPARTMENTAL DITTIES AND BARRACK ROOM BALLADS	*Doubleday, Doran*
THE SEVEN SEAS	*Doubleday, Doran*
THE FIVE NATIONS	*Doubleday, Doran*
SONGS FROM BOOKS	*Doubleday, Doran*
THE YEARS BETWEEN	*Doubleday, Doran*
COLLECTED VERSE	*Doubleday, Doran*

JOHN MASEFIELD

JOHN MASEFIELD

THERE is the Masefield of robust legend, the Masefield whose brief service as assistant barkeeper in a New York saloon has been magnified into a symbol of a wild, adventurous life. There is, on the other hand, John Masefield, the distinguished poet, presented for the degree of Doctor of Letters at Yale as "sailor boy, painter of the thrill and terror of the sea; singer of rural England and of the West Country which gave him birth; writer of sonnets and ballads, of tragedies, of novels; analyst of the agonies of sin, the heights and depths of human passion; historian of British deeds in 'the arts of war that sickle men like wheat,' and patriot and poet."

Greater than either of these, because including both, is the real John Masefield. The clew to this Masefield, he himself gives in two of his poems, "A Consecration" and "Biography." In the latter he records those elements that have gone into his own creation: "Those moments of the soul in years of earth." He recalls

> The night alone near water when I heard
> All the sea's spirit spoken by a bird,

some swift vision of the countryside, a glimpse of a Roman ruin, full-sailed ships, "men, hard-palmed," London friends, and hours of toil—all those instances which showed him happy visions of a world greater than this world.

> Best trust the happy moments. What they gave
> Makes man less fearful of the certain grave,
> And gives his work compassion and new eyes.
> The days that make us happy make us wise.

But "Biography," by itself, is not sufficient to explain the man. Because his poetry is so much a part of him, "A Consecration" is needed to complete his picture. His poetry, Masefield declares, will sing of "the men of the tattered battalion which fights till it dies."

Masefield is, then, at heart a romanticist, seeking in people and events evidences of something finer and better than this world offers. But he looks at them with the eyes of a realist, willing to see the evil with the good, the ugly with the beautiful; and it is as a realist that he describes them in his poetry.

The effort to fill in with specific details this outline of biography and personality may lead to the fate that the poet deplores, of having all his thoughts and deeds "reduced to lists of dates and facts." Yet dates are not without value in binding incidents together; and the gleam of important moments need not be lost because those moments are chronologically arranged. True, which incidents were most significant to the poet, the poet alone can tell; but those which his poetry suggests will be better understood if they can be referred to the known facts of his objective life.

It was on June 1, 1878, at the Knapp, Ledbury, Herefordshire, that John Edward Masefield was born, the son of a solicitor, George Edward Masefield, and Caroline Louise Parker. While the boy was still very young, both his parents died; and he with the other Masefield children went to live with an aunt at the Priory in Ledbury. He attended the local Ledbury school.

There must have been a number of "golden instants and bright days" in his childhood. Books provided many of them. He recalls now two stories that he read when he was about seven: one, the story of a man and a woman in a deserted oil town in America; the other, "The War Trail," by Captain Mayne Reid, discovered in *Chambers Journal* one spring Sunday evening when he was left alone in the house. At ten he was learning the stories of England's past through Scott's poems and through Percy's *Reliques of Ancient Poetry;* at fourteen, the legends of a still more distant past through Macaulay's *Lays of Ancient Rome.* He knew *Hiawatha* and *The Ingoldsby Legends;* and Thomas Hood's "I Remember" he had learned by heart to please his mother.

One effect of his reading was to stir his imagination to the telling of stories. This ability was discovered at school and often called upon by fellow pupils. Another and natural result of his reading was to arouse in him the desire to create poems. "I do not remember writing verses in my childhood," he says in the preface to the 1918 collection of his work. "I made many, but I did not write them down. ⏤ remember writing two poems when I was nine years and nine months old, one about a pony called Gipsy and the other about a Red Indian."

Neither school nor literature, however, absorbed all his time. He had a venturesome spirit, which he indulged by running away from school and home, tramping the countryside far and wide. Somewhere among his wanderings, whether escorted by his family or not is not known, he encountered examples of two very old forms of English drama. One, several hundred years old, was the Christmas mummers' play of *St. George of Cappadocia*, a very short play followed by a dance, which was produced by rough country laborers. The other, which he saw on a hill in the wild country near Wales, in a place that "seemed haunted by the very beginning of England," had its origin in that early beginning. It was a brief folk drama, a ritual preceding the killing of an ox. It is at least possible that from these two survivals of early English plays came Masefield's intense interest in poetic drama and his conviction of the close relationship between poetry and the race.

However valuable the boy's wanderings may have been for gathering impressions that were to make the man and poet, his family seemed to feel that some curb on them was needed. So at fourteen he was sent to the training-ship *Conway*, to undergo the discipline and to learn the trade of a sailor. For three years, on that boat and in the regular merchant service, he sailed the seas, experiencing the harshness of the ocean, reveling in its beauties. He came to know the sea; and he came to know sailing ships with the real knowledge of a common sailor. "I just went to sea," he said once in a talk at the Seamen's Institute in New York, "in time to see the single topsail and the stu'ns'l boom, those terrible tormentors of poor seamen." But in spite of the hard work, he loved the sea and felt it answering a need of his soul. Its beauty and majesty color all his poetry, provide him with the material of *Dauber*, an epic of the sea, and provoke his cry, as in "Sea Fever":

I must go down to the seas again, to the lonely sea and the
    sky,
And all I ask is a tall ship and a star to steer her by,
And the wheel's kick and the wind's song and the white
    sail's shaking,
And a grey mist on the sea's face and a grey dawn
    breaking.

And with the sea he came to know and love those who followed it. He knew men not as their officer, but as their fellow worker; he shared their loyalties and their joys; he experienced with them their toil and privations. Their life was hard. "In those days sailors were not treated either well or badly. They weren't treated at all, but neglected." These were the workers whose laureate he was to be in *Salt Water Ballads*.

But life on shipboard, glamorous though it was at those moments when the sea revealed some new beauty or when the boat touched at some strange port, was not wholly satisfying. For Masefield soon realized that he wanted to write, and the life gave him too little chance for the study he knew was necessary for his writing. So when he was not yet seventeen, he gave up for good the career of a sailor; and early in April 1895 with five dollars, a chest of clothes, and a desire to write he landed in New York.

He lived in Greenwich Village, sharing a garret room with two other men. "We reduced our expenses to tenpence a day among the three of us. We did our own washing and dried it out of the window. One of us slept each night on the floor upon a pile of newspapers, with a coat for a pillow." He did all sorts of odd jobs to earn some money, worked in a bakery, a livery stable, and along the water front.

One night he dropped in at the bar of the Columbian Hotel at 5 Greenwich Street, now destroyed to make room for a New York subway, and asked for work. The hotel owner, Mr. Luke O'Connor, made him an assistant bartender and put him to cleaning glasses and keeping the icebox filled. He won the confidence of his employer and was invited to eat his meals with his employer's family in their flat about a half-mile away from the café. And there, it is said, he at times took care of the O'Connor baby to Mrs. O'Connor's complete satisfaction.

One day, after about four months of barkeeping, a man named Quinn, with whom Masefield was then living, introduced him to Mr. William Booth from Yonkers. Mr. Booth was attracted to the young man, asked him if he wanted a good job, and told him he could get him one in a Yonkers carpet factory at $1.05 a day.

So early one morning Masefield left New York for Yonkers. Something of his life there is told in an article by Louise Townsend Nicholl in *The Bookman* for January 1919; and concerning the work itself, she quotes Masefield:

"At first I worked with a tin-opener, a little instrument like a fork without tines, to keep straight the tin tubes on the spools of wool from which the carpets were woven. If this were not done, the carpets were irregular. I used to do 40 sets in a day, for 40 carpets. Then I got a raise, and finally crept up to $8.50 a week. And then I was made mistake-finder, to take a strip of new carpet and compare it with the pattern, for faults of 'setting' or design."

For two years "Jack" or "Macy" worked at the factory. For some of this time he lived with one of the factory men; for the rest, at a Mrs. White's where Billy Booth also lived. Mr. Booth was one of the very few people who in this period were at all close to Masefield. "Jack was very retiring," he says, "a bashful fellow. He had an idea that he wanted to take up medicine, but he didn't want to write to his uncle in England to ask for any help." Mr. Booth undertook the task of writing, but no help was forthcoming.

The desire to be a doctor seems, however, to have been a temporary one. More permanent and much stronger was the desire to write; and the life that fulfilled this desire may be said to have begun for Masefield in Yonkers. For here he first studiously applied himself to reading as preparation for his life-work.

Friday in the factory was pay day. Fridays, after work, Masefield hurried to the bookshop of Mr. William Palmer East to buy a book to read over Sunday. His first book was a volume of Chaucer. "I did not begin to read poetry with passion and system until 1896," he writes. "I was living then in Yonkers, New York (at 8 Maple Street). Chaucer was the poet and *The Parliament of Fowls* the poem of my conversion. I read *The Parliament* all through one Sunday afternoon, with the feeling that I had been kept out of my inheritance and had suddenly entered upon it, and had found it a new world of wonder and delight. I had never realized, until then, what poetry could be." Keats and Shelley followed Chaucer, all in books costing seventy-five cents apiece; then Shakespeare, Swinburne, and Rossetti. For prose he read De Quincey, Hazlitt, Dickens, Kipling, Stevenson, and Sir Thomas Browne. He managed to give to his reading two hours each night, five hours on Saturday, and the whole day on Sunday.

Mr. East became interested in his customer. He had long talks with him; realized how broad-minded he was; and noted his "sane unprejudiced view of kings and lowly men."

Suddenly the Yonkers life ended. On July 4, 1897, Masefield took passage home. For a long time no word came from him to his American friends. Later they learned that he had not had enough money to buy stamps!

On his return to England, he lived in the Bloomsbury section of London and found there as one of his friends the Irish dramatist Synge. His London residence was interrupted by six months' work on *The Manchester Guardian,* a period of which little more is known than that it confirmed his reputation for being reserved.

Back in London, his literary apprenticeship over, Masefield published in 1902 his first book of poems, *Salt Water Ballads*. The poems were poems of the sea, vivid pictures of men and of boats, told in the language of sailors, and in a manner suggesting Kipling.

At this time, Masefield's life must have been bright with many "gleams." For he spent a summer in Devonshire with William Butler Yeats, the Irish poet, who was to influence his writing and of whom he afterwards said, "But I owe everything to Yeats. What glory there is is due to him." And in 1903, he married Constance De La Cherois-Crommelin, to whom he dedicates one after another of his books and of whom he wrote such tender lyrics as "Her Heart" and "Beauty":

I have heard the song of the blossoms and the old chant
    of the sea,
And seen strange lands from under the arched white sails
    of ships;
But the loveliest things of beauty God ever has showed to
    me,
Are her voice, and her hair, and eyes, and the dear red
    curve of her lips.

From this time, too, Masefield's literary career became well founded. Yet he seemed not to have decided definitely what form it was to take. In 1903 he published *Ballads*, a collection of well and delicately wrought poems, many of them showing in their mood the influence of Yeats. Yet poetry did not appear with any certainty to be his inevitable medium. For he wrote short tales of ships, such as *Mainsail Haul;* and a study of the sea, *Sea Life*

in Nelson's Time; boys' books, like *Martin Hyde, the
Duke's Messenger;* novels, like *Captain Margaret, Mul-
titude and Solitude,* and *The Street of Today;* plays, like
The Tragedy of Nan and *The Campden Wonder;* and
literary studies, like *Shakespeare.*

Nineteen hundred and eleven, however, made it clear
that though Masefield was thereafter to write an occasional
novel or a drama, it was preëminently as a poet that he was
to be considered. In that year *The English Review* published *The Everlasting Mercy,* thereby establishing Masefield's literary position and, at the same time, stirring up
such a storm of controversy as had seldom before been
aroused. There is no surer way of realizing the liberalization of poetry both as to material and as to method since
1911 than to recall that this story of the conversion of the
poacher Saul Kane, with its fight and its tavern rioting,
provoked such language of criticism as "violence" and
"licentiousness." Some saw in it, only to condemn, descriptions of low, mean characters not the fit subject of poetry,
and epithets and expressions that English gentlemen
simply did not use. Others, however, recognized a fresh
note in English poetry and gloried in the poem's physical
and spiritual exaltation. After an intoxicated celebration
of his victory over Bill Myers, Saul Kane hears the church
bells ring:

> The bells chimed Holy, Holy, Holy:
> And in a second's pause there fell
> The cold note of the chapel bell,
> And then a cock crew, flapping wings,
> And summat made me think of things.

His change of heart, however, does not take place immediately. After further carousing, a wild race through the
town, an argument with the parson, and after insulting the
Quaker Miss Bourne and being rebuked by her, Saul
finally goes out into the country:

> All earthly things that blessèd morning
> Were everlasting joy and warning.

He sees Callow, the plowman, and realizes that as a
plower he, too, will find peace with God:

> There came such cawing from the rooks,
> Such running chuck from little brooks,
> One thought it March, just budding green,
> With hedgerows full of celandine.
> An otter out of stream and played,
> Two hares came loping up and stayed;
> Wide-eyed and tender-eared but bold.
> Sheep bleated up by Penny's fold.
> I heard a partridge covey call;
> The morning sun was bright on all.
> Down the long slope the plough team drove,
> The tossing rooks arose and hove.
> A stone struck on the share. A word
> Came to the team. The red earth stirred.
>
> I crossed the hedge by shooter's gap,
> I hitched my boxer's belt a strap,
> I jumped the ditch and crossed the fallow;
> I took the hales from farmer Callow.

That was true poetry, Masefield's defenders maintained.
And for it the Royal Society of Literature awarded him
the Edward de Polignac Prize of £500. The poem was
the first of Masefield's work to be published in America.

There appeared in rapid succession three more long
narratives: *The Widow in the Bye Street* (which had been
written before *The Everlasting Mercy*), *Dauber*, and *The
Daffodil Fields*. *The Widow in the Bye Street* is the story
of a mother whose only son falls in love with an unworthy
woman, murders the woman's lover, and is finally condemned to death. Throughout the tragedy the mother's
love is triumphant. In *The Daffodil Fields* also two men
quarrel over a woman and by a twist of irony kill each
other, although their difficulty was on the point of being
solved.

There is another suggestion of irony in *Dauber*, the
story of the sea and the story of a man's soul. With the
vividness of his own experience, Masefield narrates the
voyage of a ship around the Horn; he depicts life on
board; he describes with convincingness the days of calm
weather and with awful intensity the storm:

> Darkness came down—half-darkness—in a whirl;
> The sky went out, the waters disappeared.
> He felt a shocking pressure of blowing hurl
> The ship upon her side. The darkness speared
> At her with wind; she staggered, she careered,
> Then down she lay. The Dauber felt her go;
> He saw his yard tilt downwards. Then the snow

Whirled all about—dense, multitudinous, cold—
Mixed with the wind's one devilish thrust and shriek,
Which whiffled out men's tears, deafened, took hold,
Flattening the flying drift against the cheek.
The yards buckled and bent, man could not speak.
The ship lay on her broadside; the wind's sound
Had devilish malice at having got her downed.

It is in that storm that Dauber proves himself. Dauber
has left his father's farm for shipboard, impelled by a desire to paint the sea:

It's not been done, the sea, not yet been done,
From the inside, by one who really knows.

That he may learn to paint

the men and rigging, and the way
Ships move, running or beating, and the poise
At the roll's end, the checking in the sway—

he endures the hardships of a sailor's life and the taunts of
the crew who have no sympathy with his desire; he suffers,
too, the torments of his own soul because he is afraid that
he may show his fear of the sea. But in the great storm,
Dauber overcomes his dread; he climbs the rigging and
helps furl the sails. He wins the respect of the crew. And
when again the call comes "All hands on deck!" Dauber
is the first to appear.

Any other poet might here let Dauber go on with his
painting. But Masefield must give a touch of irony and
must show the triumph of man's soul over physical de-

feat. As the boat nears harbor, Dauber is sent once more to climb the mast. He slips, falls, and breaks his back. He has learned ships but he is never to paint them. Yet it is not with a note of hopeless tragedy that he dies: " 'It will go on,' he cried aloud, and passed."

With these four poems, Masefield's fame was secure as the poet of the English country, of the sea, and of lowly men who knew spiritual triumphs. He wrote other plays and other poems that were well received.

And then in 1914 began the great war. All that the cataclysm meant to him, all that it meant to England, all that it meant to humanity, he expressed in his poem, "August, 1914." He shows the beauty and peace of the countryside, the young men leaving for war and dying for a vague but strongly felt ideal. Any hope of immortality, he feels, must be bound up with these "men and things we love."

Masefield's contact with the war and its fighters was not merely the contact of a poetic imagination. In August 1915, after several months' experience in French war hospitals, Masefield left for the Dardanelles in charge of a picket boat and barge for conveying the wounded from Gallipoli.

In January 1916 he came to this country, his first visit here in twenty years. He came to note conditions here and the effect upon the American people of enemy propaganda. He found that there was great need for counter-acting lies about the Gallipoli campaign. On his return to England, the government gave him the job of clarifying

JOHN MASEFIELD

the erroneous impression. The result was his book *Galli-poli*, a modern *Chanson de Roland*, a thrilling narration of the campaign in the Dardanelles, an ardent eulogy of troops gallant in defeat.

The British War Office then sent him to France to examine the relief work being conducted by American organizations. In Paris, he met a member of the British Military Commission and was introduced to General Haig. General Haig appointed him to the official post of historian and sent him to the Somme theater of the war, where he saw the battle of October 1916. After going to England to give his report on American relief, he returned once more to the Somme battle-front and stayed there from January until June 1917. The results of his observations he published in *The Old Front Line*.

In January of the next year, he arrived again in America, this time to make a lecture tour of American camps as a representative of the British Pictorial Commission. The talks he gave have been gathered together in two books: *The War and The Future* and *St. George and The Dragon*.

The war proved to be no swiftly passing interlude in Masefield's life. It affected his point of view and so his poetry. His roots seemed to go deeper into England, and he to become more dearly and more permanently attached to his English country. He seemed to identify himself more closely with the race of Englishmen, to have a fuller social sense. This attitude apparently gave him an answer to the question arising from those many individual deaths he had seen in war. The death of the individual is rela-

tively unimportant; what is significant is the continuity of
work, the continuity of the race.

In *Sonnets* and in *Lollingdon Downs*, published during
the war, there is a seeking for the answer to the riddle
of life:

> What is this atom which contains the whole,
> This miracle which needs adjuncts so strange,
> This, which imagined God and is the soul,
> The steady star persisting amid change?

This search for that truth which Masefield comes to identify with beauty and with wisdom is never completely successful; its answer is sometimes suggested, but never
definitely revealed:

And when the hour has struck, comes death or change,
Which, whether good or ill, we cannot tell,
But the blind planet will wander through the range
Bearing men like us who will serve as well.

But in his post-war poems, Masefield turns from intro-
spection and finds his inspiration in English life, and in his
fellow Englishmen. *Reynard the Fox*, *Right Royal*, and
King Cole are of the English country and essentially of
groups of English people.

Reynard the Fox is the story of a hunt, in which the fox
is the hero. "I wrote *Reynard the Fox*," Masefield says
in the introduction to his poems, "partly because the events
of a fox hunt have been for some centuries the deepest
pleasure in English country life, and partly because the fox

hunt brings together on terms of equality all sorts and conditions of the English people."

The sympathy that he here extends to animals is again manifested in *Right Royal*, the glorification of the English sport of the steeplechase, wherein Masefield suggests the subtle relation between horse and rider. A third English activity, the traveling circus, is the subject of *King Cole*. This of the three has the richest spiritual content and in its supernatural—and charming—return to this earth of the legendary king carries Masefield back to the past of England.

In *Midsummer Night*, Masefield again finds his inspiration in England's past, this time as chronicled in the tale of King Arthur; and again he touches his poems with magic and the supernatural by introducing the legend that on summer nights Arthur and his court return to the world of mortals for a few hours before daybreak. This book appeared as recently as 1928.

Meanwhile, he had written *Enslaved* and *The Dream*, had translated two plays of Racine, and had written two more novels, *Odtaa* and *Sard Harker*.

Meanwhile, too, he had paid still another visit to America, coming here in 1926 to lecture on poetry, which was "only to give myself an excuse for a pleasure trip."

What manner of man is this lecturer? He is tall and lean. He has a finely shaped head with a lower jaw that suggests great strength. But it is his eyes that dominate his face. Blue, wistful, almost mystical, they give a gentle and reflective impression without, however, destroying any of the effect of masculinity. "But if you expect to find him human," wrote John Cournos in *The Independent* for September 5, 1912, "you will find him abnormally human."

Since his marriage in 1903, Masefield's home has been in England, for a time in Great Hampden near London and, at present, at Boar's Hill, Oxford, where his gardens look down upon the university. There he has had built a model theater seating about one hundred, in which the Boar Hill Players (his daughter Judith among them) present plays. So Masefield the mature man and recognized poet is linked to the little boy who saw an ancient English drama produced on a rugged western hill. For in stimulating interest in the drama and particularly in poetic drama, Masefield is furthering the project so close to his heart, the bringing together again, as once they were in the past, of poetry and the people.

It was as an evidence of this interest that he wrote *The Coming of Christ*, a mystery play that was produced in Canterbury Cathedral. And in furtherance of this interest he has taken an active part in The Association for Speaking of Verse, an association which, holding annual competitions at Oxford, has for its purpose the fostering of a love for spoken poetry freed from slovenliness of speech and artificialities of diction and gesture.

In an address, *With the Living Voice*, delivered on October 24, 1924, at the first general meeting of the Scottish branch of the Association, Masefield outlined the development of the relationship between poet and people. "To most simple communities," he said, "poetry is the gift of the gods which fills out and makes radiant this life of

ours"; and again, "Poetry is always wanted; it is a need
of the human heart." But most significant is his statement,
"The life and thought about us must be the foundation
of our life and thought." For it is in the life and thought
about him, in the reality of his own experience, that he
most successfully finds the inspiration of his poetry, rather
than in abstract thought—at which he does not seem happy
—or in imaginative wanderings; and this experience he
transmits in definite pictures, in concrete images. He recognizes two purposes in art, an "elaboration of artifice" and
"a greater closeness to reality." For himself, he definitely
chose the latter.

It is not that he rejects all artifice or is inexpert in the
technical devices of the poet. His earlier poems were carefully wrought pieces, designed as the perfect expression
of his thoughts and feelings. Such a poem is "The West
Wind."

Will you not come home, brother? You have been long
    away.
It's April, and blossom time, and white is the spray;
And bright is the sun, brother, and warm is the rain,—
Will you not come home, brother, home to us again?

Another is "Cargoes":

    Quinquireme of Nineveh from distant Ophir,
    Rowing home to haven in sunny Palestine,
    With a cargo of ivory,
    And apes and peacocks,
    Sandalwood, cedarwood, and sweet white wine.

Stately Spanish galleon coming from the Isthmus,
Dipping through the Tropics by the palm-green shores,
With a cargo of diamonds,
Emeralds, amethysts,
Topazes, and cinnamon, and gold moidores.

Dirty British coaster with a salt-caked smoke stack,
Butting through the Channel in the mad March days,
With a cargo of Tyne coal,
Road-rails, pig-lead,
Firewood, iron-ware, and cheap tin trays.

This poem, concentrating, as it does, three complete
civilizations into three symbols, suggests Masefield's manner of translating his thoughts and experiences into pictures and suggestive imagery. He has great skill in presenting a convincing picture with an economy of expression:

> I saw a mighty bay's wind-crinkled blue
> Ruffling the image of a tranquil town.

Or

> The loitering water, flooded full,
> Had yeast on its lip like raddled wool,
> It was wrinkled over with Arab script
> Of eddies that twisted up and slipt.

Just so, in a line, he can draw the picture of men: "Eye-
puckered, hard-case seamen, silent, lean."

This power of portraiture is particularly well displayed
in the first part of *Reynard the Fox*, when the people of

the hunt are presented one after another, individually, unforgettably.

When he deals with men, he uses their proper speech, the language of the hunt, of the stable, of the country, and —undeniably—of the sea. "Sing a Song O' Shipwreck" and "Burial Party" are ample proof of that. So when Saul Kane in *The Everlasting Mercy* uses ungentle language, it is not because Masefield enjoys coarseness; it is rather because as a realist he is striving to give the same verisimilitude to a tavern scene that, by having his characters talk of square sennits and of staysails, he gives to a sea scene.

There are, it is true, occasional inconsistencies of language. The mother in *The Widow in the Bye Street* may say at one time:

> He used to stroke it, did my pretty son,
> He called it Bunny, little Jimmy done;

and, at another:

> God dropped a spark down into everyone,
> And if we find and fan it to a blaze
> It'll spring up and glow, like—like the sun,
> And light the wandering out of stony ways.

But these are not so much indications of failure to know how such characters talk, as they are evidences of the presence of Masefield, the romanticist, who sees in these characters something more than they present to the casual world.

As in diction, so in meter and verse form, Masefield displays craftsmanship. He can suggest the varying movements of a boat, and he can, by his meter, re-create the rapidity of a horse race. He produces well-executed sonnets and variations of the seven-lined rhyme royal and eight-lined and nine-lined stanzas, with complicated rhyming schemes.

It is quite evident, then, that the artifices of poetry are completely within his power. Yet because he has chosen for himself that other function of the poet, the closer approach to reality, he sometimes becomes negligent as a writer. For the sake of meter, definite and indefinite articles are calmly omitted, or old forms of words incongruously introduced, as *newë* for *new*. Lines are sometimes halting: "I'll want no tomb but what the parish gives." "Mother, I lied to you that time, O forgive." Nor is it difficult to find careless rhymes, not simply in the conversation of characters whose mispronunciations might serve as explanation, but in the lines of the poet speaking as himself. *Banners* is made to rhyme with *bandannas, trees* with *primroses*. One other weakness should, perhaps, be noted, a loose and sometimes formless handling of plot in his narratives.

The total effect, however, is not one of weakness, for individual incidents are vivid and gripping: Saul Kane saying good-by to his mother, Right Royal taking a ditch, or Reynard finding the burrow stopped with stones. One is willing to sacrifice well-knit plot for these.

For there is no question that Masefield can tell a moving, a thrilling, story. Besides the longer narratives already mentioned, there are the ballads, "The Yarn of the *Loch Achray*," "The Wanderer," the stories of "The River," "The Hounds of Hell," and the tales in *Midsummer Night*, particularly "The Fight on the Wall," "The Fight at Camlan," "Dust to Dust," and "South and East," any one of which will hold the reader's interest and stimulate his imagination.

Throughout Masefield's poetry one finds a deep love for the English country, a country of primroses, of dim woods, of farmers, and of shepherds. "Tewkesbury Road" sounds the call to enjoy its delights; *The Daffodil Fields* is filled with descriptions of its beauties:

Still as high June, the very water's noise
Seemed but a breathing of the earth; the flowers
Stood in the dim like souls without a voice.

King Cole gives it its full expression:

And then, as in the spring when first men hear,
Beyond the black-twigged hedge, the lambling's cry
Coming across the snow, a note of cheer
Before the storm-cock tells that spring is nigh,
Before the first green bramble pushes shy,
And all the blood leaps at the lambling's notes,
The piping brought men's hearts into their throats.

The note of mystery, of the supernatural, is one closely connected with the sea and its sailors. There are frequent references to the superstitions of the sailors: in "Burial Party," to the belief that corpses should not be buried at night; In "Sea-Change," to the belief that sea gulls are the souls of dead mariners; and in "Cape Horn Gospel," to the reputed disappearance of ghosts at cockcrow.

Such superstitions might, it is true, be gathered from any book on nautical life. But in Masefield's poems there is the feeling of authenticity and vividness that makes one realize that this knowledge comes from intimate contact with men, not from books about them. So, knowledge and experience of the life on board ship are unhesitatingly felt to be the basis of poems like "Fever Ship," "Fever-Chills," and "Evening—Regatta Day," poems of men who work and suffer.

There is no hint of lack of sincerity in Masefield's attitude toward men. He knows them and feels with them. They are, as he presents them, victims of an inscrutable power, pawns moved by some hand—"The dark, invisible hand of secret Fate." Irony enters frequently into their lot. But what if fate, and ironic fate at that, results in apparent defeat? Men in such defeat are then most glorious: "Made half divine to me for having failed." For, says Masefield, it is not so much the defeat or the victory that is important; it is the activity, the "delights of work most real." For work continues beyond the lifetime of the individual:

"And there we'd talk how little death would be,
Knowing our work was going on here still."

This delight in humanity, this zest for life, its activity and its dangers, are the basis of Masefield's philosophy and lead to the beauty which is the goal of his seeking. What the ultimate answer to his questioning search is, one can not be entirely sure; if he himself knows, he never quite reveals it in his poetry. One feels, however, the romanticist's hints of a world finer than this one; suggestions that the poet makes in his article "Contemplatives":

"But if we have faith, we measure life by the great event, and count as specially lived those days about the great event when we had suggestions of something bigger than ourselves, suggestions of reality, beauty, and order."

POETICAL WORKS

STORY OF A ROUND-HOUSE AND OTHER POEMS
The Macmillan Company

THE EVERLASTING MERCY AND THE WIDOW IN THE BYE STREET *The Macmillan Company*

PHILIP THE KING AND OTHER POEMS
The Macmillan Company

GOOD FRIDAY AND OTHER POEMS
The Macmillan Company

LOLLINGDON DOWNS AND OTHER POEMS
The Macmillan Company

POEMS *The Macmillan Company*

REYNARD THE FOX, OR THE GHOST HEATH RUN
The Macmillan Company

RIGHT ROYAL *The Macmillan Company*

KING COLE *The Macmillan Company*

THE DREAM AND OTHER POEMS
The Macmillan Company

ENSLAVED AND OTHER POEMS
The Macmillan Company

SELECTED POEMS *The Macmillan Company*

A KING'S DAUGHTER, A TRAGEDY IN VERSE
The Macmillan Company

THE COLLECTED WORKS OF JOHN MASEFIELD
The Macmillan Company

Volume I. Poems
Volume II. Poems
Volume III. Verse Plays

SALT WATER POEMS AND BALLADS
The Macmillan Company

TRISTAN AND ISOLT   *The Macmillan Company*

THE COMING OF CHRIST   *The Macmillan Company*

MIDSUMMER NIGHT   *The Macmillan Company*

SOUTH AND EAST   *The Macmillan Company*

ALFRED NOYES

ALFRED NOYES

" ALFRED NOYES, ambassador," is what the poet
might very aptly be called, although no reference
book and no official biography thus names him. He has, it
is true, received his ambassadorial credentials from no
country with definite boundaries. Still he has represented a
very real, if somewhat hazier, realm. For he has been an
ambassador of poetry to a people scornful or suspicious
of the art; he has made poetry popular. But, more than
that, to those grown old he has been ambassador of myth,
of fairyland, and of childhood.

> O, grown-ups cannot understand
>   And grown-ups never will,
> How short's the way to fairy-land
>   Across the purple hill:
> They smile: their smile is very bland,
>   Their eyes are wise and chill;
> And yet—at just a child's command—
>   The world's an Eden still.

And at the same time, he has been an ambassador of simple
truth and faith to those bewildered by the complexities
of life. "Our world is now so highly specialized," he says,
"that it grows more and more difficult for us to relate our

particular fragment of the truth to the whole. For great art, great literature, great poetry, enable us, once more, to see all things in one."

It is not difficult to reconcile these two apparently contradictory aspects of his rôle. For Alfred Noyes has enlarged fairyland to include the whole world; he looks upon the universe with wonder and delight; he imagines himself fairy-small so that he may realize

> How fraught each fragrant bough would be
> With dark o'erhanging mystery.

It is with a fairy-like directness, a childlike optimism and faith that he reaches his conception of reality, his belief in a God who created the universe as a harmonious whole, whose laws—however unfathomable to man—exist and govern logically.

Like a true ambassador, Noyes does not permit his mission to become obscured by a cluttering of small personal details; his poems are more significant than dates or incidents in his life. He was born September 16, 1880, the eldest son of Alfred Noyes and Amelia Adams Rowley. His home was near Chapel Ash, Wolverhampton, Staffordshire in England; but he left it as a young boy to return to it only on rare holiday visits. His childhood, to judge from his poems, must have been rich with books, with imaginative wanderings, and with a love of the country. A delightful picture of what might well have been the pleasures of his early years is given in his poem, "To a Friend of Boyhood Lost at Sea":

ALFRED NOYES

Old friend, do you remember yet
The days when secretly we met
    In that old harbor years a-back,
Where I admired your billowing walk,
    Or in that perilous fishing smack
What tarry oaths perfumed your talk,
    The sails we set, the ropes we spliced,
    The raw potato that we sliced,

For mackerel-bait—and how it shines
Far down, at end of the taut lines!—
    And the great catch we made that day,
Loading our boat with rainbows, quick
    And quivering, while you smoked your clay
And I took home your "Deadwood Dick"
    In yellow and red, when day was done
    And you took home my Stevenson?

This joyous interest in the sea, that he here suggests,
was to continue with him always. A second interest manifested itself in science, particularly in astronomy. "The
story of scientific discovery had always fascinated me,"
he writes in "A Mountain Observatory," "from the nights
when—as a schoolboy—I used to climb out on the roof
and try to chart the stars between the chimney pots with
the aid of a very small telescope."

Poetry was a third interest, beginning in childhood and
never for a moment deserting him. As a child of nine he
recognized this interest in a desire to write a poem. At
fourteen, he wrote his first epic, a poem of several thousand lines describing life as a voyage on a ship. This poem

he sent to James Payne, the novelist, who returned it with a sympathetic and encouraging letter and with the suggestion that the young poet read a great deal more and not try to publish anything for a number of years.

The kindly sympathy was appreciated; for it was to Payne that Noyes in 1902 dedicated his first book, *The Loom of Years*. And the advice was doubtless followed. For Noyes was nineteen when his first poem was published —"The Symbolist," printed in the *London Times*. Meanwhile, he had gone to Oxford, to Exeter College. There he rowed number six on the college eight. There he read widely, becoming familiar with the long tradition of English poets. And there he, himself, wrote many poems.

He had a rich conception of poetry as a force that analyzes mankind's various activities, evaluates them, and, binding them together again, presents them as reflections of the soul of the universe. To further such a purpose was a worth-while ambition. So Noyes resolved to give his life to poetry, to make poetry his profession. He was determined, moreover, that that profession should earn him his livelihood. After leaving Oxford, he contributed poetry to many English periodicals, to the *Spectator*, the London *Bookman*, *The Outlook*, *The Speaker*. Mr. R. C. Lehmann, who reviewed Noyes's first book of poems for *The Speaker*, was most enthusiastic and introduced the young poet to the editor of *Blackwood's Magazine*. Thereafter, *Blackwood's* proved a cordial host and much of Noyes's later poetry was printed first in that magazine.

The Loom of Years was favorably received by others besides the reviewer of *The Speaker*. It called forth generous praise from Meredith and from Swinburne. The poet was well on the road to fame. He was a prolific writer and his volumes of poems followed each other in quick succession, bringing him to the popular attention of English and American readers, who welcomed this teller of tales in singing meters and rhymes. The English and American editions of his poetry differ in content and in names. The latter includes three volumes of *Collected Poems*, a complete edition of his work to 1920, *Dick Turpin's Ride*, and two volumes of his trilogy, *The Torch-Bearers—Watchers of the Sky* and *The Book of Earth*. Noyes has, in addition, edited several anthologies of poetry; written a number of short stories; and published two volumes of critical essays, *Some Aspects of Modern Poetry* and *New Essays*.

Included in the American *Collected Poems* is *The Flower of Old Japan*. This volume, published in England in 1903, won for the poet an invitation to attend the London meeting of the Japan Society. Yet his knowledge of Japan was purely the knowledge of imagination, such knowledge as one might win from old willow-tree-patterned plates. His epic tale, *Drake*, also included, gives another interesting light on his literary method. That poem had appeared serially in *Blackwood's Magazine*, quite an unusual procedure for a poem. But still more unusual was the fact that the first sections appeared before the poem had been half completed and its second half was written from month to month. It was this poem that helped make Noyes's fame secure.

By 1913 people on both sides of the Atlantic knew

and loved "The Barrel-Organ," "The Highwayman,"
"The Flower of Old Japan," "The Forest of Wild
Thyme," and the "Tales of the Mermaid Tavern." That
year the American admirers had an opportunity to see
for the first time the creator of the poems. In February,
Noyes arrived in this country. He came, at the invitation
of the Lowell foundation, to lecture on "The Sea in
English Poetry." There was, however, an additional
reason for his coming. His wife, whom he had married in
1907, was an American, Miss Garnett Daniels, the daughter of one of General Grant's officers, Col. B. G. Daniels;
she was eager that her husband find in her native country
new inspiration for his poems.

America received Noyes cordially and discovered in
him a new kind of poet. There was about him no suggestion of a long-haired, pale eremite wooing his muse in a
garret; instead there was a clean-shaven, alert, smiling
individual who seemed like nothing more mysterious than
a very energetic, athletic business man!

But this business-like poet came with a poet's message
for the nations of the world. "My aim, which may be regarded as merely a poet's idealism," he said, "is the even-
tual setting up of a centralized court of arbitration." Poetry
and peace, then, was the purport of his message; and in
the six weeks' tour that took him as far west as Chicago,
he lost no opportunity of making clear his position. He
urged the disarmament of nations; but this disarmament,
he realized, must be gradual and evolutionary. That belief in slow modification rather than in revolutionary
upheaval is important; for it dominates every field of his

thought—religion, art, politics. The past must not be discarded, he maintains; it is needed, link forged to link, to make sure the present.

His first visit was highly successful. He received the honorary degree of Litt.D. at Yale. And he created throughout the United States a demand for his work and for himself. In October of 1913 he returned for a six months' trip. Before all sorts of groups he lectured on poetry and—with an almost prophetic sense of the war about to break out—on the subject of international peace. He visited the colleges of the country and stimulated in their students a keen interest in poetry.

In the spring of 1914 it was announced that Noyes had been elected a visiting professor at Princeton. As Professor of Modern English Literature he was to lecture one term in each academic year in the senior course on Nineteenth Century English Literature. In an interview in the *New York Times* for March 18, 1914, he spoke of the college student and poetry. Poetry is not a thing apart from life, he said; "the poet must use his imagination to bring people into touch with life." Poetry is essential to an understanding of life; "if you eliminate poetry, you shut up twenty gates to knowledge." Poetry, he went on to explain, must not be limited to the few; it is democratic in its appeal and there is a democratic reason for its appreciation. "The basis of poetry—the basis of all arts—is the sense of rhythm, and the sense of rhythm is universal."

From 1914 to 1923 Noyes as a professor at Princeton expounded his views. He was a popular lecturer and made his subject popular. "Having a poet for a professor removes your awe of poetry," said one student. E. A. Cook in *The Bellman* describes him in the classroom:

"The men who sat in Mr. Noyes's classes could find nothing of the freakish or the esoteric in the alert, well-set-up young man who faced them. He was not a recluse; he did not pose; he did not cultivate any eccentricity of dress or manner. Just as his presence served to dispel a false awe of poetry, so did his personality convince his students that an enthusiasm for poetry, and hard muscles, masculine initiative and intellectual sanity might coexist."

This same picture of simplicity and geniality is given in a recent description of him [1] by St. John Adcock, the editor of the London *Bookman*.

"Of all poets I have met none is more easily unself-conscious than Noyes. He is tall, upright, sturdy of figure and rather suggests the capable man of business who keeps up his health and vigor on the golf links. He has no pose, no eccentricities of any sort; if there are no artificialities in his verse it is because there is none in himself. His features in repose may be grave and a little severe; he is a good talker and can talk of the highest, gravest matters without ever being portentous, but in general converse he will handle an argument doughtily, playing fair as a listener, or gossip lightly on occasion with a shrewd sense of humor and a ready laugh that, like himself, is genial and kindly."

In the summer following Noyes's professorial appointment, the great war broke out. The poet of peace devoted

---

[1] "The Homer of Science," New York *Herald Tribune*, July 8, 1928.

himself passionately to England's service. It was not that
he forswore his earlier ideals; it was, rather, that he saw
the only possibility of their fulfillment in the victory of
England and her allies. Three times Noyes tried to enlist
in the British army, but because of his eyesight he was
rejected. Furthermore, it was felt that he could accomplish
more as a writer defining England's position and ideals
than possibly he could as a soldier. In 1916 he was tem-
porarily attached to the Foreign Office. In 1918, in recognition of the value of his work, he was made a Commander
of the Order of the British Empire.

He saw in the war a moralizing force. "The war,"
he said, "is bringing us right up against things that we
have been ignoring, such as ethics and religion." Still, it
overwhelmed him and seemed to have, for a time at any
rate, a devastating effect upon his poetry. The foundation of Noyes's universe was law, manifesting itself in
orderly evolution. War was a contradiction, an infraction
of that law; and something not easily to be placed within
the scope of his philosophy.

Nevertheless, with faith he clung to his ideals. Nor did
he once relinquish his hope of a lasting universal peace.

During those years, after the end of the war, when
the relationship between England and America needed
redefinition, Noyes served to interpret America to his
native land. In his trips through this country he had visited
more than one hundred and fifty institutions and more
than six hundred towns and cities, so that it was from no
slight or superficial contact that he spoke. "One of the
chief causes of international misunderstanding," he wrote,

"is the habit of generalizing on inadequate grounds." So in a series of articles reprinted in *New Essays and American Impressions* he explains America to his countrymen. With Anglo-American friendship and peace, his ideal must be somewhat nearer fulfillment!

Aside from his views on questions of public importance, details of his personal life are few. In 1927 he received the degree of LL.D. from Glasgow University. In the same year, after the death of his first wife, he married Mrs. Richard Weld-Blundell, the widow of an English officer. He lives in London, in a home overlooking Regents Park.

This scarcity of information concerning Noyes's personal life is significant and consistent with his attitude that it is the social, rather than the personal, aspect of the poet that is important. Moreover, since he believes in the poet as universal interpreter, it is only natural to feel that the views he delivers in his articles and from the lecture platforms are reflected in his poems and that these poems can be best understood in the light of his theory of poetry.

Poetry for Noyes "is the revelation of the abiding beauty behind the transient." It must have the rhythm and the beat of music; it must be something that can be remembered. Furthermore, it is based on the past; and it is based on law. "There is an absurd idea today that genius is opposed to law. It is often opposed to arbitrary pedantries; but on law, in the larger and nobler sense, its very life depends." This law is continued in unbroken succession. "There is neither new nor old. There is poetry."

This theory put into practice results in poetry that is simple and straightforward. It contains no very great subtleties; it is never unduly intellectualized. In method it carries on the tradition of the English poets of the past. Noyes is unalterably opposed to radicalism, and particularly to radicalism in verse, which he sees as an effort to upset necessary and logical laws.

"Touchstone on a Bus" expresses his contempt for the rebel against laws and conventions:

> They are hawking a new rose for Eden.
> It has feathers. It's green. I suppose
> The only thing wrong with their rose is
> The fact that it isn't a rose.
> Who'll buy?
> And here's a new song without metre;
> And, here again, nothing is wrong
> (For nothing on earth could be neater)
> Except that it isn't a song.

But if Noyes did not ally himself with the "new poetry," which he felt was formless, he did experiment with the old poetic forms, and succeeded in creating new rhythms and effects. In what new patterned forms Noyes cast .his verse is suggested by such poems as the Prelude to "The Forest of Wild Thyme," or "A Song of Sherwood":

Sherwood in the twilight, is Robin Hood awake?
Grey and ghastly shadows are gliding through the brake,

or "The Day of Remembrance":

Dazzle of the sea, azure of the sky, glitter of the dew on
    the grass,
  Pass to Oblivion
    In the darkness
With all that ever is or ever was.

Noticeable in Noyes's verse is a spondaic effect, an
effect which gives weight and emphasis to a line. This he
achieves by the actual introduction of a spondee, a foot
made up of two long syllables, as in the second foot of
the line: "On the broad black breast of a midnight lake."
Or, as is much more frequent, he achieves it by omitting
the unaccented syllable from one or more of the feet in
a line. Two typical examples are:

Friar Tuck and Little John are riding down together
With quarter-staff and drinking-can and grey goose-
    feather.

Across the seas of Wonderland to Magadore we plodded,
Forty singing seamen in an old black barque.

Even in so formalized a meter as blank verse, Noyes
introduces modifications. His long blank-verse narratives
are interspersed with delicate lyrics in totally different
meters; and even the narrative itself may be punctuated
with lines that vary from the required iambic pentameter:

His dumb stare told the rest; his head sank down;
He strove in agony
With what all hideous words must leave untold.

In Book XI of *Drake,* the verse alternates between blank verse and a rhymed stanza, now one, now the other, to suggest the opposing movements of the English and the Spanish squadrons.

Perhaps nowhere is this flexibility of rhythm better expressed than in "The Barrel-Organ." Quotations of isolated lines will illustrate nothing. The poem should be read in its entirety to see how the meter changes to suggest the various songs the organ plays and the thoughts of the London people who hear its songs. Yet the result is unity; for there is a singleness of theme and the parts are held together not only by the repeated line—"In the City as the sun sinks low"—but by that undercurrent repetition of the mechanical unwinding of the organ's music roll:

Come down to Kew in lilac-time, in lilac-time, in lilac-
    time;
    Come down to Kew in lilac-time (it isn't far from
    London!)
And you shall wander hand in hand with love in summer's
    wonderland;
    Come down to Kew in lilac-time (it isn't far from
    London!)

Such verse *sings.* And that is the first verse quality upon which Noyes insists.

In rhyme, Noyes shows an equal dexterity. Nimbly he uses double rhyme and internal rhyme. Rhymes seem to come spontaneously. In any other poet "A Triple Ballad of Old Japan," for example, would seem a tour de force; in Noyes it appears as just one more evidence of skill.

Nine stanzas repeat the three rhymes of *ay*, *ow*, and *an*,
found in the opening stanza:

> In old Japan, by creek and bay,
>   The blue plum-blossoms blow,
> Where birds with sea-blue plumage gay
>   Thro' sea-blue branches go:
> Dragons are coiling down below
>   Like dragons on a fan;
> And pig-tailed sailors lurching slow
>   Thro' streets of old Japan.

In "Astrid," he tries the very interesting experiment of
initial rhyme:

White-armed Astrid—ah, but she was beautiful!—
Nightly wandered weeping thro' the ferns in the moon,
Slowly, weaving her strange garland in the forest,
Crowned with white violets,
Gowned in green.
Holy was that glen where she glided,
Making her wild garland as Merlin had bidden her,
Breaking off the milk-white horns of the honeysuckle,
Sweetly dripped the dew upon her small white
Feet."

An appealing poem, a successful illustration of original
meter and a liberated rhyming scheme, is "The Waggon":

Crimson and black on the sky, a waggon of clover
    Slowly goes rumbling, over the white chalk road;
And I lie in the golden grass there, wondering why

So little a thing
As the jingle and ring of the harness,
The hot creak of leather,
The peace of the plodding,
Should suddenly, stabbingly, make it
Strange that men die.

Only, perhaps, in the same blue summer weather,
Hundreds of years ago, in this field where I lie,
Cædmon, the Saxon, was caught by the self-same thing:
The serf lying, dark with the sun, on his beautiful wain-
load,
The jingle and clink of the harness,
The hot creak of leather,
The peace of the plodding;
And wondered, O terribly wondered,
That men must die.

"The Waggon" illustrates one of Noyes's favorite devices, the use of repetition and refrain. Sometimes it is a
line that is repeated in several stanzas: "There is a song
of England" in the poem, "A Song of England," or
"Carol of birds between showers" in "A May-Day Carol."
Sometimes stanzas are used as refrains, as in "The Barrel-
Organ." Frequently a stanza, either the opening or the
second one, is repeated as the final stanza of a poem.
Such a use, when it is least successful, suggests that the
poet's fervor has worn out before the poem's completion
and can be recaptured and revived only by repetition.
When it is successfully employed, however, sometimes

with a change in a word or phrase, it adds roundness and emphasis.

Such a successful use of the device is made in "The Progress of Love":

> In other worlds I loved you, long ago:
>   Love that hath no beginning hath no end.
> The woodbine whispers, low and sweet and low,
> In other worlds I loved you, long ago;
> The firwoods murmur and the sea-waves know
>   The message that the setting sun shall send.
> In other worlds I loved you, long ago:
>   Love that hath no beginning hath no end.

That stanza opens the poem and closes it; and, within itself, shows the use of repetition.

Somewhat akin to repetition, in the sense of familiarity that it provokes, is Noyes's incorporation into his poems of allusions or quotations. The old skeptic, in the poem of that name, sees once more the old faith:

And the strange old light on their faces who hear as a
    blind man hears,—
  Come unto me, ye weary, and I will give you rest.

The "Forest of Wild Thyme" echoes Tennyson's poem:

                              That dead poet's cry—
  "Little flower, but if I could understand!";

it also repeats Shakespeare's fancies: *"I know a bank where the wild thyme blows"*; and with its delightful modifications of the nursery rhyme, of Ladybird, Cock

Robin, Little Boy Blue, The Spider and the Fly, turns
again the pages of Mother Goose.

The allusive value of such quotations adds a richness
to the poems that is further increased by the lavish use
of color and by the rapid passage of suggestive details,
as in the curious crowding of a dream:

> *There with a hat like a round white dish*
> *Upside down on each pig-tailed head,*
> *Jugglers offer you snakes and fish,*
> *Dreams and dragons and gingerbread;*
> *Beautiful books with marvellous pictures,*
> *Painted pirates and streaming gore,*
> *And everyone reads, without any strictures,*
> *Tales he remembers for evermore.*

It is this sense of a glowing and full canvas that one
is more likely to recall than any single, sharply drawn
picture. But occasionally an image is penned with indelible
strokes. There is, for example, "trotting rain," and there
is the song of a city "that was like a blazoned missal-
book." "The Shining Streets of London" becomes a vivid
picture:

> Busses (with coloured panes that spill
> A splash of cherry or daffodil)
> And lighted faces, row on row,
> From darkness into darkness go.
>
> *O Love, what need have you and I*
> *Of wine and palm and azure sky,*
> *And who would sail for Greece or Rome*
> *When such a highway leads him home?*

The subjects which lend themselves to Noyes as material for poetry are not necessarily the conventionalized subjects of the older poets—busses, coffee stands, tramps, did not appear with any frequency in their lines. But the treatment which he gives to them is traditional poetic treatment; they are made to shine with the glamor of fancy and romance. A newsboy becomes an "elf of the city"; and of an electric train, Noyes writes: "And the lightning draws my car tow'rds the golden evening star." One hears throughout his poems, however modern and of this world the subject, the poet's call:

> Fairies, come back! We have not seen
> Your dusky foot-prints on the green
> This many a year.

This particular combination of material and method leads frequently to a curious mixture of seeming non-sense and profound truth. The episode of the spider in "The Forest of Wild Thyme" is an illustration of this, or "A Spell (An Excellent Way to Get a Fairy)." For a complete example, there is "The Tramp Transfigured." Bill, the tramp, who lies in the fields and earns an occasional penny by selling bunches of cornflowers at Brighton, becomes the glorified character of a fairy tale: "Me that was a crawling worm became a butterfly." While he is endowed with the fairy qualities—perhaps it was only a dream, what then!—of transformation and of wealth mysteriously increasing, he becomes the instrument of a meeting after twenty years of absence between a very

unfairy-like mother and her son; and, while he tells the
tale of his whimsical adventure, he becomes the mouth-
piece of a meaningful philosophy:

What if there should be
One great Power beneath it all, one God in you and me?

The incongruity of ideas in this poem becomes the
source of humor, rich and kindly, a vein of humor that
is carried on in "Bacchus and the Pirates" and in "Forty
Singing Seamen" who were puzzled by the problem:

Could the grog we *dreamt* we swallowed
Make us *dream* of all that followed?

Whether it be with humor or pathos, with wistfulness
or direct energy, that Noyes presents his material, the
variety of his moods is outnumbered by the variety of
his subjects. Classical mythology, history, science, nature,
philosophy—these all become the material for poems.
Frequently, they are given a lyric treatment, as the love
song of "The Return," or the country song of "A Devonshire Ditty," or the fancy of "Our Lady of the Twilight."

But however charming Noyes may be when singing
his lyrics, he is happiest when telling a tale and creating
the atmosphere for a story. "The Highwayman" is an
example of compression and of rapid movement of in-
cident; "The Admiral's Ghost," of the mystery and supernatural to be found in a folk ballad.

This narrative skill leads frequently to an epic and
dramatic handling of the material of the past. This past,

for Noyes, may be either the past of an individual—his childhood and his childhood fancies, as in "The Flower of Old Japan" and "The Forest of Wild Thyme"—or the past of a race, the tapestry of English history, as in "Sherwood."

By means of Oberon and Titania, Noyes introduces the fairy element into this dramatization of the story of Robin Hood and Maid Marian. The most touching character of the play, Noyes's particular contribution to Robin Hood legend, is Shadow-of-a-Leaf, Marian's fool who, for love of his mistress, tells his fairy secrets and so foregoes his own chance of entering fairyland:

> Never to join our happy revels,
> Never to pass the gates of fairyland
> Again, but die like mortals.

England's historical, as well as legendary, past gives Noyes inspiration for many poems. Particularly successful are the nine making up the *Tales of the Mermaid Tavern*. Whether or not these are historically accurate pictures is a matter of indifference; at all events, they possess poetic verity and satisfactorily re-create the Elizabethan spirit and the spirit of the group of frequenters at the Mermaid Tavern that numbered among its members Marlowe, and Jonson, and Shakespeare. These do more than create atmosphere; they tell good stories, whether it be the whole-hearted, humorous tale of "Black Bill's Honeymoon," or the gentle one of "The Companion of a Mile," the familiar story of Dick Whittington in "Flos Mercatorum," the tragic death of Marlowe in "The Sign of the Golden Shoe," or the supernaturally moving one of "The Burial of a Queen."

Underlying these tales is the implication that the characters are more than people passing through adventures. They are, for Noyes, manifestations of England's greatness, forces contributing to the working out of England's destiny. This belief in England, this passionate devotion, colors almost all of Noyes's poetry. There are poems, like "Nelson's Year," "The Peacemaker," "To the Memory of Cecil Spring-Rice," "The Union," that were inspired by specific events and that prompted the suggestion in 1913, after the death of Alfred Austin, that Noyes be made Poet Laureate. There are poems that sing the love of the English country, poems like "A Devonshire Ditty," "The White Cliffs," "On the South Coast," "The World's May Queen"—

> When Spring comes back to England
> And dons her robe of green,
> There's many a nation garlanded
> But England is the Queen.

These poems are made up of the flowers, and birds, the lanes, and the hedgerows of England. But most important as a symbol of England's position and of England's purpose is the sea; and the most important poem of England's greatness is *Drake*, the epic of the sea. However *Drake* may be criticized because of its structure, its loosely organized plot, its introduction of a personal love motif into the story of a nation, it nevertheless remains a sweeping tale of grandeur, with moving, thrilling incidents. Unforgettable is the scene of Doughty's execution as a traitor; or the scene at the church when Drake's love, Bess of Sydenham, refuses to marry the man her father chose; or the final fight between Drake and the Spanish fleet. The story of *Drake* is more than the tale of a conquering buccaneer; it is a panegyric of England as the champion of righteousness. Yet it is no confining patriotism that motivates Noyes. England is to be a liberating force, and her ideals are to embrace the world.

Peace between nations is, naturally, the first step toward the achievement of Noyes's goal; and peace between England and America lies very close to his heart. So he interprets America to his countrymen; so he writes poems like "Princeton" and "The Mayflower" to suggest the ties that bind these two nations. From this understanding he would have a universal peace develop. The peace that he idealizes is not merely a laying down of arms between nations; it is, rather, one that comes from the righting of all human wrongs.

It might seem unwise to place too heavy a burden of philosophy upon the poems of Alfred Noyes. When Noyes is most concerned with the logical, reasoned exposition of his philosophy, he is least successful as a poet. He is most successful when his poems are touched by his imagination and carry only an implied message. It is not for his philosophy that one returns to Noyes, but for his moving narratives, light with rhyme and rhythm.

For a time it seemed that the fame of Noyes would rest not upon the general coördinated body of his verse, but upon some dozen or so individual poems, those poems that were popular when he first came to this country. But such an opinion must now be modified. In *The Torch-Bearers* he is creating a work that in plan and in method throws light upon and epitomizes his previous writing.

"The story of scientific discovery," Noyes says in the preface to the first volume of *The Torch-Bearers*, "has its own epic unity—a unity of purpose and endeavor—the single torch passing from hand to hand through the centuries; and the great moments of science when, after long labor, the pioneers saw their accumulated facts falling into a significant order—sometimes in the form of a law that revolutionized the whole world of thought—have an intense human interest and belong essentially to the creative imagination of poetry."

The theme was long in the poet's mind. But the first volume, *Watchers of the Sky*, began to take definite shape when Noyes saw the first trial of the one-hundred-inch telescope at the Mt. Wilson Observatory in California. This volume tells the story of astronomy; the second, *The Book of Earth*, tells the story of the evolutionary interpretation of creation, the story of geology and biology; the third, not yet completed, is to tell the story of discovery in physics.

The method used is the method of the "Tales of the Mermaid Tavern." In a flexible blank verse, interspersed with occasional lyrics, the intellectual adventurers from Copernicus to Sir John Herschel and from Pythagoras to Darwin are made to live again in the narratives of their achievements. Tycho Brahe in his observatory, Sir William Herschel conducting his orchestra, Leonardo da Vinci talking to the painter, Linnæus and his students, Darwin on his boat the *Beagle,* touched by a magic touch, are brought to life from the pages of textbooks.

These stories have an essential unity. All the characters are on the same quest that Drake was on, that the children in "The Forest of Wild Thyme" pursued. And in their quest for truth, each realizes the dependence of his work upon the work of his predecessor and its importance for those who are to come after him. Each holds the torch of knowledge and hands it on:

> Take thou the splendour, carry it out of sight—
> Into the great new age I must not know,
> Into the great new realm I must not tread.

It is the same insistence that has been noticed before; the insistence upon the past as essential to the present, upon gradual and evolutionary development.

The truth which these torch-bearers find is not the truth of disillusionment, of negation, or of blind chance. It is the truth of faith, faith in a universe of harmonious law, in a law of love, in God.

> New every morning the creative Word
> Moves upon Chaos. Yea, our God grows young.
> Here, now, the eternal miracle is renewed;
> Now, and for ever, God makes heaven and earth.

Fairyland, heaven—call it what you will—lies about us. This is the message of Noyes, the ambassador of poetry. Beauty and song he brings to those who will listen, and to those who will believe, love and an abiding faith.

POETICAL WORKS

COLLECTED POEMS   *Frederick A. Stokes Company*
Volume I:
  The Loom of Years
  The Flower of Old Japan
  The Forest of Wild Thyme
  Forty Singing Seamen
  Drake
  A Triple Ballad of Old Japan
Volume II:
  The Enchanted Island
  Sherwood
  Tales of the Mermaid Tavern
Volume III:
  The Wine Press
  A Belgian Christmas Eve
  The Lord of Misrule
  A Salute From the Fleet
  The New Morning
  The Elfin Artist

THE TORCH-BEARERS   *Frederick A. Stokes Company*
  Watchers of the Sky
  The Book of Earth

DICK TURPIN'S RIDE   *Frederick A. Stokes Company*